The Untold History
of the Fuji School

The Untold History of the Fuji School

The True Story of Nichiren Shoshu

By the SGI-USA Study Department

World Tribune
Press

Published by World Tribune Press
606 Wilshire Blvd., Santa Monica, CA 90401

© 2000 Soka Gakkai

ISBN 0-915678-76-4

Design by Gary Ross

10 9 8 7 6 5 4 3 2

Editor's Notes

The SGI-USA Study Department wishes to acknowledge the publication *Ankoku no Fuji Shumonshi Nikken Shu no Engen o Kiru* (The Dark History of the Fuji School: Revealing the Origins of the Nikken Sect; Tokyo: Daisanbunmeisha, 1997) by Hajime Kawai, vice senior advisor of the Soka Gakkai Study Department. Much of the content in *Untold History of the Fuji School* is taken from that source.

Throughout the text, sources that appear frequently are abbreviated as follows:
- WND refers to *The Writings of Nichiren Daishonin* (Tokyo: Soka Gakkai, 1999).
- LS refers to *The Lotus Sutra* (trans. Burton Watson; New York: Columbia University Press, 1993). In this case, "LS" precedes the chapter number and then the page number.
- GZ refers to *Nichiren Daishonin Gosho Zenshu* (Tokyo: Soka Gakkai, 1953).

Contents

Foreword

One of the most crucial lessons I've learned from the temple issue over the past nine years is the importance of developing a strong, independent faith. Rather than relying on interpretations, including those of the Nichiren Shoshu priesthood, this issue has caused me to return to Nichiren Daishonin's teachings like never before and to strive to understand his heart. I'm sure I'm not alone when I say that, in this sense, the temple issue has been a great benefit, a powerful cause for advancement. And, along with all of you, my education continues, not only in learning about the Daishonin's compassionate and courageous spirit but in learning the role of religion as we enter the twenty-first century.

A part of this education has been to take a hard look at history, for as the philosopher wrote, "Those who cannot remember the past are condemned to repeat it." The current circumstances did not arise recently or out of a vacuum. The roots of the issue can be traced back centuries to the time soon after the Daishonin's death and can be attributed to human foibles and the darker side of human nature. This look at history reveals the priesthood to be, as Phillip Hammond and David Machacek state in their book *Soka Gakkai in*

America, "a product of feudal Japanese culture—an era when values of duty, loyalty, obedience, and tradition reigned." In one sense, the story here is not all that new—it has been repeated in many religions throughout the world.

The priesthood's history, as is so evident on these pages, is one of self-preservation, compromised beliefs and utter misunderstanding of the Daishonin's will. Even as a person who grew up and was educated in Japan, I never knew the details of that history until I read this account, first serialized in *Living Buddhism.* Reading it has made so many aspects of this issue clear to me for the first time, and for that I am grateful to all who made that series and this book possible.

We of the SGI, with our own history to learn from, have the ultimate responsibility to propagate this Buddhism. By reading this historical account, we can help clarify for ourselves the essence of this temple issue and can resolve in our hearts not to repeat any of these past mistakes. And with a selfless practice, deep conviction and a profound awareness of our mission, let us make Nichiren Daishonin's Buddhism a religion for the people in the twenty-first century.

Daniel Nagashima
SGI-USA General Director

Introduction

To most SGI members, the corruption of the Nichiren Shoshu priesthood first came to light when its plot to destroy the SGI surfaced at the end of 1990. However, the root cause of the priesthood's present corruption and turmoil dates back much further. The priesthood did not suddenly become aberrant. It has always had such a tendency, which became most evident when Nikken Abe, the sixty-seventh high priest of Nichiren Shoshu, initiated his plan to disband the SGI and bring its members over to his temples.

Josei Toda, the second president of the Soka Gakkai, knew well of this tendency. "In the seven-hundred–year tradition of this school," he once said, "there were, on one hand, some who were noble, pure and worthy of respect. But, on the other hand, you may find others like cats or rats." Throughout Nichiren Shoshu's history, many high-ranking priests, including some high priests, distorted Nichiren Daishonin's Buddhism and sought personal gain by using their religious status and authority.

Until recently, only certain events in the history of Nichiren Shoshu—the so-called Fuji School of Nichiren Buddhism—could be discussed. These included Nikko Shonin's founding of Taiseki-ji (Nichiren Shoshu's head temple); the selfless dedication of the third high priest, Nichimoku, to spread the Daishonin's Buddhism; the restoration of the school by the ninth high priest, Nichiu; the establishment of the school's doctrinal foundation by the twenty-sixth high priest, Nichikan; and the sect's unprecedented development after World War II thanks to the Soka Gakkai. In reality, however, "the pure stream of the Fuji School," as the priests liked us to call it, was sporadic at best. The rest of the Fuji School history could best be described as "a muddy stream."

The fifty-ninth high priest, Nichiko Hori, an eminent scholar of Nichiren Daishonin's Buddhism, lamented the widespread corruption within the priesthood. He once satirically said: "It has fallen upon my ears that the wise priests of the Latter Day— throughout their past, present and future existences—always keep this thought in mind: 'How can I cause my purse to acquire money quickly?' How could this be possibly true?" (*One Hundred Sacred Admonitions* [Jpn *Seikun Ippyaku Dai*], p. 22). Here, of course, he was paraphrasing the famous conclusion of the Lotus Sutra's "Life Span" chapter: "How can I cause living beings to . . . quickly acquire the body of a Buddha?" (LS16, 232).

While Nichiko pointed out that within the priesthood there have always been corrupt priests living off Buddhism, the current situation is worse than ever. Now that the high priest himself has strayed from the Daishonin's Buddhism, corruption has spread throughout the priesthood, affecting greater numbers than ever before.

When we examine the entire seven-hundred-year history of the priesthood, we can see that distortion of the Daishonin's Buddhism and corruption are not new. The sect's history contains numerous precedents to the current corruption. Understanding the priesthood's history, therefore, gives us an invaluable insight into the current temple issue and is an excellent opportunity to deepen our understanding of the Daishonin's Buddhism.

CHAPTER 1

The Deviations of the Five Senior Priests

The history of the Fuji School, founded by Nikko Shonin, began when he departed from Kuon temple at

Nikko Shonin's Departure From Mount Minobu

Mount Minobu. Because of his deep understanding of the Daishonin's teachings and his courageous action to propagate it despite numerous persecutions, Nikko Shonin inherited the Daishonin's spiritual legacy. In fact, the Daishonin had entrusted Nikko Shonin with "the Law that Nichiren propagated throughout his lifetime" and referred to him as "the great leader of the propagation of true Buddhism" (GZ, 1600). The Daishonin also called this outstanding disciple "a chief priest of Kuon temple at Mount Minobu" (GZ, 1600).

So why did Nikko Shonin feel compelled to leave Mount Minobu where his teacher had spent his last years?

The direct cause of Nikko Shonin's departure from Mount Minobu lies in the so-called four slanderous acts of Hakiri Sanenaga, the steward of Minobu. Hakiri contradicted the Daishonin's teachings in four ways:

• He had a statue of Shakyamuni made and regarded it as

an object of devotion.

• He visited a Shinto shrine.

• He made an offering to a stupa[1] of the Nembutsu sect.

• He built a place of religious practice for the Nembutsu sect.

Although Nikko Shonin strongly admonished Hakiri for his errors, he would not listen.

Regarding these errors, the fifty-ninth high priest, Nichiko Hori, points out: "Of the four slanderous acts, the gravest is his restoration of the Buddha's statue" (*Detailed Accounts of Nikko Shonin of the Fuji School*, p. 218). Viewing Shakyamuni's statue as an object of devotion goes against the Daishonin's essential teaching that the Gohonzon is the basis of our faith and the fundamental object of devotion. Because of the gravity of Hakiri's behavior, Nikko Shonin refused to compromise.

In his letter "Reply to Mimasaka-bo," Nikko Shonin recounts the Daishonin's last will and testament: "When the steward [of Minobu] goes against the Law, I shall not reside here" (*Hennentai Nichiren Daishonin Gosho*,[2] p. 1729). Following the Daishonin's last instruction and to protect the integrity of Buddhism, Nikko Shonin moved to the Fuji area.

Behind Hakiri Sanenaga's slanderous acts was the influence of Niko, chief priest of the seminary at Minobu. Sanenaga had been converted to the Daishonin's Buddhism by Nikko Shonin, so he regarded him as a teacher in the beginning. But when Nikko Shonin admonished the steward's behavior, he replied, "I have taken Minbu Ajari [Niko] as my teacher" (ibid., p. 1733).

Aware of the circumstances under which Sanenaga committed these slanderous acts, Nikko Shonin states in "Reply to Lord Hara": "These things are not the fault of lay priest

[Hakiri]. They are solely the errors of the twisted priest" (ibid., p. 1733).

Niko propounded that "When those upholding the Lotus Sutra visit [a Shinto shrine], the Buddhist deities as well will come to that shrine" (ibid., p. 1732). However, in his treatise "On Establishing the Correct Teaching for the Peace of the Land," the Daishonin states that when people ignore the Law, all the Buddhist deities (i.e., the protective forces in the universe that protect life) will abandon the land so that people's misery and suffering will increase.

Based on the Daishonin's teaching, Nikko Shonin discouraged believers from visiting a Shinto shrine. But Niko allowed believers to visit them and criticized Nikko Shonin, stating that "Byakuren Ajari [Nikko] reads only non-Buddhist scriptures and is ignorant of the ultimate teaching of Buddhism" (ibid., p. 1732).

Niko deviated both in his understanding of Buddhism and in his behavior. In "Reply to Lord Hara," Nikko Shonin describes Niko's aberrant behavior: Niko invited a painter to the estate of lay priest Moro'oka and had him paint a mandala. To consecrate the painted mandala, he gave a sermon for one day and one night and then got drunk on sake while holding fast to the offering he received for performing the consecration. Furthermore, heavily drunk, he sang vulgar songs and made a laughingstock of himself. Regarding Niko's disgraceful behavior, Nikko Shonin writes: "What could possibly bring more shame upon Nichiren than this?" (ibid., p. 1734).

Commenting on this statement, Nichiko Hori states: "We priests and lay believers of the modern day must deeply understand his statement and regard it as golden words with which to admonish ourselves. We must not take these words lightly, thinking of them as empty words from six-hundred-some years ago" (February 1956, *Daibyakurenge,* p. 3).

Of the six senior disciples designated by the Daishonin, all except Nikko Shonin betrayed their teacher's will, thereby nearly destroying his teaching. On

The Five Senior Priests' Betrayal

October 8, 1282, five days before his death, the Daishonin designated Nissho, Nichiro, Nikko, Niko, Nitcho and Nichiji as "main disciples" but noted that "the order of listing is irrelevant" (*The Collected Essential Writings of the Fuji School*, vol. 8, pp. 2–3). The order of the Daishonin's designation indicates the order of conversion, not the order of seniority.

These "main disciples" were later called "the six senior priests." The Daishonin designated the six senior priests under the leadership of Nikko Shonin to protect and spread his teachings after his death. While designating Nikko Shonin as chief priest of Kuon temple at Minobu, the Daishonin also intended the other five senior priests to continue to take leadership in their assigned areas for the further propagation of the Law. As Nichiko Hori later wrote, the Daishonin "asked them to become leaders for believers scattered in various areas and exert themselves in propagation, thus accomplishing the great desire of kosen-rufu."

On October 13, 1282, the Daishonin died at the estate of Ikegami Munenaka. His body was cremated, and Nikko Shonin brought the ashes back to Minobu for burial. At the end of January 1283, after having conducted a memorial service for the hundred-day anniversary of the Daishonin's passing, Nikko Shonin consulted other disciples and instituted a vigil for their teacher's grave at Minobu. Eighteen leading disciples were selected to take turns attending the grave by making offerings and prayers.

Each of the six senior priests and two of the rest were to stay at Mount Minobu for one month at a time and protect the Daishonin's gravesite. Of the eighteen priests, nine (Nichii, Nippo, Echizen-ko, Nitchi, Nichiji, Nichimoku, Nisshu, Nichiben and Nikke) had entered the priesthood under the guardianship and guidance of Nikko Shonin, demonstrating his outstanding leadership.

When the disciples eventually returned to their respective areas, Nissho took with him an annotated copy of the Lotus Sutra, which the Daishonin had instructed to keep by his tomb. And Nichiro took a statue of Shakyamuni, which the Daishonin had received as a gift from the steward of Ito when he was exiled to Izu and had since kept by his side. The Daishonin had also willed this statue to be kept by his tomb. Nissho and Nichiro never returned to Minobu as long as Nikko Shonin remained there, completely neglecting the vigil over their teacher's grave.

In his "Reply to Mimasaka-bo," Nikko Shonin explains his circumstances: "[The five senior priests] seem to have abandoned the grave [of the Daishonin]. Though they propounded a teaching not to discard one's teacher, they have already abandoned their own. It cannot be helped that they may be subjected to criticism in the secular world" (*Hennentai Nichiren Daishonin Gosho*, p. 1729).

When Nikko Shonin became chief priest of Kuon temple, Hakiri Sanenaga, the steward of Minobu, rejoiced: "I am pleased as if the late sage had come back once again" (*Detailed Accounts of Nikko Shonin of the Fuji School*, p. 164). But after Niko was designated as head of the seminary at Minobu in 1285, Hakiri gradually came under his influence.

Niko would not hesitate to bend the Daishonin's Buddhism to curry favor with Hakiri, which eventually led to slanderous acts.

The five senior priests could not support Nikko Shonin and thus betrayed the Daishonin's teaching, because they were jealous of him. Their ill feelings toward the Daishonin's foremost disciple eventually clouded their perspective and led them astray.

Jealousy Toward Nikko Shonin

Of the five senior priests, Nissho and Nichiro became disciples of the Daishonin before Nikko Shonin had. To them, Nikko Shonin was a junior priest. Niko and Nitcho joined the Daishonin's order after Nikko Shonin, but they considered themselves his equals in status and seniority. Nichiji entered the priesthood under the guidance of Nikko Shonin, but he disliked obeying his senior. Their jealousy and emotionalism clouded their judgment so much that they eventually stopped visiting Minobu and started to propound their own teachings.

Besides jealousy, the five senior priests' cowardice and ignorance of the Daishonin's Buddhism also played a role in their betrayal. After the Daishonin's passing, Nissho and Nichiro—who lived in Kamakura, the seat of the shogunate government—were oppressed by the government, which threatened to destroy their temples. They managed to escape from this predicament by offering to pray for the government based on the Tendai sect's practice. Fearing persecution and eager to preserve their security and social status, they curried favor with the government while compromising their teacher's will.

The five senior priests' shallow understanding of Buddhism

and weak faith led them to believe that the Daishonin was spreading the Lotus Sutra based on the Tendai doctrine. In this regard, Nikko Shonin explains: "The five senior priests proclaimed that Sage Nichiren's teaching is that of the Tendai school, so they called themselves in their letters submitted to the government 'the followers of the Tendai school'" (GZ, 1601). They also allowed their junior priests to receive the precepts at the Tendai school's head temple at Mount Hiei (GZ, 1602).

The five senior priests' betrayal of the Daishonin's teaching was detailed in Nikko Shonin's writings such as "On the Matters That the Believers of the Fuji School Must Know" (GZ, 1601–09) and "Refuting the Five Senior Priests" (GZ, 1610–16). According to Nikko Shonin's account, the five senior priests' errors can be summarized as follows:

1) They asserted that the Daishonin's teachings belong to the Tendai school, and that he spread the teaching of the Lotus Sutra following the teaching of Dengyo.

2) They visited Shinto shrines in places such as Ise, Mount Izu, Hakone and Kumano.

3) They regarded copying of the Lotus Sutra as a legitimate practice and encouraged it.

4) They allowed their disciples to enter the priesthood and receive the precepts at the Tendai sect's head temple at Mount Hiei.

5) They called the Daishonin's letters written in the common language of the time (Japanese phonetic characters) their teacher's shame and destroyed them.

6) They made a statue of Shakyamuni and regarded it as an object of devotion.

7) They disrespected Gohonzon inscribed by the Daishonin,

hanging them behind Shakyamuni's statues, leaving them in a corridor, burying them with bodies or selling them off for profit.

Not only did the five senior priests go against the Daishonin's teaching, but they also slandered Nikko Shonin for admonishing their errors. As Minobu school scholars acknowledge in *The Doctrinal History of the Nichiren Sect,* there was nothing remarkable in the five senior priests' Buddhist study. They grew weak in faith, became fearful of persecutions, became oblivious to the Daishonin's desire to spread the Law and eventually completely strayed from the Daishonin's teaching. These characteristics shared by the five senior priests are applicable to those who betrayed Buddhism throughout its history.

In the document entrusting Kuon Temple at Mount Minobu to Nikko Shonin (dated the thirteenth day of the tenth month in the fifth year of Koan [1282]), the Daishonin states: "The teachings expounded by Shakyamuni for fifty years I have transferred to Byakuren Ajari Nikko. He shall be chief priest of Kuon Temple at Mount Minobu. Those who betray him, be they lay believers or priests, shall be known as slanderers of the Law" (GZ, 1600). When the five senior priests started opposing and denouncing Nikko Shonin, they further proved themselves to be slanderers of the Law.

In "Letter from Sado," the Daishonin also warns his followers of the treachery of priests against Buddhism: "Neither non-Buddhists nor the enemies of Buddhism can destroy the correct teaching of the Thus Come One, but the Buddha's disciples definitely can. As a sutra says, only worms born of the lion's body feed on the lion" (WND, 302). The Daishonin's premonition came true soon after his passing. The five senior priests, as "the Buddha's disciples," attempted to destroy their teacher's work from within. As the Daishonin points out, throughout the history of Buddhism, its decline and corruption have been caused by priests, especially those of high status. The history of the Nichiren Shoshu priesthood is no exception to this historical pattern.

The five senior priests' betrayal of the Daishonin is instructive for those of us practicing today. Nikko Shonin's resolute and uncompromising efforts to refute the five senior priests' erroneous teachings and clarify believers' confusion may be regarded as examples of

The Five Senior Priests and Today's Nichiren Shoshu Priesthood

how a true Buddhist acts.

As Nichiko Hori has said: "The flow of the Law of Nichiren Daishonin is frequently obstructed. Obstacles arise from both within and without, but those from within inflict the most serious wounds. . . . With external obstacles, even if they interrupt the flow [of kosen-rufu], it will revive again after a period. With internal obstacles, however, the flow is interrupted as a result of a complete drying up [of the flow itself], thus it is not as easy to revive. Unless we all profoundly recognize this point, the prospects of seeing the dawn of kosen-rufu even in a thousand or ten thousand years will be extremely dim."

The treacherous nature of the five senior priests corresponds to the basic tendency of the current Nichiren Shoshu priesthood. Just like the five senior priests seven hundred years ago, today's priesthood has completely strayed from the Daishonin's teaching. Its denial of the equality of lay believers and priests; its attempt to insert it-self between believers and their enlightenment by claiming control and authority over the Gohonzon; and its view of the high priest as the sole embodiment of the Daishonin's teaching—none of these principles come from the Daisho-nin's Buddhism. Furthermore, the priesthood acts like the five senior priests by being jealous and slandering the SGI, which is correctly carrying on the Daishonin's will just as Nikko Shonin did.

A parallel can also be drawn between Nichiren Shoshu's head temple, Taiseki-ji, which has degenerated into a slan-derous place, and Mount Minobu, which became a slander-ous place because of the actions of Hakiri Sanenaga. That's why Nikko Shonin left Mount Minobu, the place where his teacher had spent his last years. Similarly, Taiseki-ji, under the control of Nikken, has turned into a place of slander.

While the Dai-Gohonzon that was bestowed upon the entire world remains the basis of our faith, to donate money to Nikken in order to see the Dai-Gohonzon would amount to condoning his slander of the Law. Supporting slanderous priests in this way would mean being guilty of the same of-fenses they are.

To use a metaphor, the "Former Affairs of the Bodhi-sattva Medicine King" chapter of the Lotus Sutra likens the sutra to "a clear cool pond [that] can satisfy all those who are thirsty." Today, we can say that the Dai-Gohonzon is the "clear cool pond." But the area surrounding this pond is a swamp of slander. To reach the pond, one must travel through the swamp. So while the pond is still every bit as clear as before, because of the surrounding swamp, one's life will be muddied when he or she tries to approach it.

Continuing with the same analogy, the water that feeds

the pond also feeds the spring that is the Gohonzon in our own homes; there is no difference at all between the water of the pond and that of the spring.

In the Daishonin's Buddhism, what connects us with our innate Buddhahood is our faith. In this sense, whether we directly pray to the Gohonzon may be considered secondary to our faith. Faith—not our physical proximity to the object of devotion—leads us to our enlightenment.

For example, the Daishonin wrote to his follower Lord Matsuno, whom he had never met: "How is it that you can have faith in Nichiren, though you have never met him? It is, no doubt, the result of good causes you have planted in your life in the past. Since the time has come when you are certain to attain Buddhahood in your next life, you now have aroused faith" (GZ, 1379). The Daishonin exclaimed how wonderful it was that Lord Matsuno had taken faith despite never meeting the Daishonin personally and assured him that he would attain Buddhahood.

Today, we could say that not to have met the Daishonin is equivalent to not having physically chanted before the Gohonzon and also, naturally, not having physically chanted before the Dai-Gohonzon. Attaining Buddhahood is not decided by externals such as meeting the Daishonin or chanting before the Dai-Gohonzon. It goes without saying that to assert that a person does not have faith unless he or she visits the head temple Taiseki-ji—as today's priests insist—contradicts the Daishonin's words.

We should look upon the Gohonzon enshrined in each of our homes as the life of the Daishonin, the entity of the original Buddha. When chanting daimoku with that conviction, it is the same as if we are worshipping the Dai-Gohonzon itself, right where we are.

As High Priest Nittatsu said: "Wherever the Gohonzon is enshrined, that place, in a broad sense, takes on the significance of the high sanctuary. The sincere daimoku you chant to that Gohonzon with a concentrated mind free of all extraneous thoughts is instantly received by the Dai-Gohonzon of the High Sanctuary of True Buddhism. The place where you chant Nam-myoho-renge-kyo is instantly transformed into Eagle Peak. And this is where you attain Buddhahood in your present form."

Nikko Shonin left Mount Minobu, a place dear to him, as an expression of his resolve never to compromise his teacher's will and intent. His departure from Mount Minobu prevented the Daishonin's Buddhism from being polluted by the five senior priests' corruption. In the spirit of Nikko Shonin, the SGI is now discouraging its members from visiting Taiseki-ji because doing so would condone the Nichiren Shoshu priesthood's erroneous claims.

No matter where we may be, as long as we pray with sincere faith, we can manifest the Buddha's life from within. The fact that SGI members throughout the world are receiving benefit from their practice is eloquent testimony to the importance of faith as taught by the Daishonin.

1. stupa: A kind of shrine in India where the relics of Shakyamuni or other saints are housed. They originated from burial mounds and are usually dome-shaped or mound-shaped.

2. *Hennentai Nichiren Daishonin Gosho*: The chronological compilation of Nichiren Daishonin's writings published by the Soka Gakkai in 1973. It also includes two letters by Nikko Shonin ("Reply to Mimasaka-bo" and "Reply to Lord Hara"), which are not in *Gosho Zenshu*. *Gosho Zenshu* is the first compilation of Nichiren Daishonin's writings published by the Soka Gakkai in 1952.

CHAPTER 2

Nikko Shonin: Protector of the Daishonin's Buddhism

Among the six senior priests appointed by Nichiren Daishonin, only Nikko Shonin proved to be a true disciple. He correctly grasped the Daishonin's intent and dedicated his life to propagating Buddhism. He viewed the Daishonin as the original Buddha of the Latter Day and understood that the teaching of Nam-myoho-renge-kyo of the Three Great Secret Laws was implicit in the "Life Span" chapter of the Lotus Sutra. The other senior priests likely viewed the Daishonin as their senior, a person with vast knowledge of Buddhism, but they appeared to lack the capacity to recognize the Daishonin's true identity and the true import of his teachings. This is the fundamental difference between Nikko Shonin and the five senior priests.

A True Disciple

Nikko became a disciple of the Daishonin in 1258 (when he was twelve years old) and, until the Daishonin's death in 1282, stayed by his side, serving his mentor and receiving instructions from him. This allowed him to read the Daishonin's treatises and letters and helped him to correctly grasp the entirety and distinction of the Daishonin's teachings.

While serving his teacher, Nikko Shonin also visited various places to spread the Daishonin's Buddhism and teach other disciples. Because of his efforts, many people started to take faith, including some priests at the Tendai sect temples Jisso-ji and Ryusen-ji in Fuji County of Suruga Province, as well as others at Shijuku-in temple in Kanbara County.

Nikko Shonin's propagation efforts, however, met with strong opposition. The chief priest of Shijuku-in, for example, persecuted those who converted to the Daishonin's teaching. The acting chief priest of Ryusen-ji, alarmed by the growing number of converts in his own parish, conspired to have twenty peasants who had taken faith in the Daishonin's teaching arrested on false charges. The believers, all from the Atsuhara district, were taken to Kamakura, the seat of the shogunate government, and interrogated by Hei no Saemon, deputy chief of the Office of Military and Police Affairs and steward of the ruling Hojo clan.

Because none of the twenty gave up their faith despite being tortured, the three leading believers (Jinshiro, Yagoro and Yarokuro) were executed and the rest banished. The three executed peasants are known in the history of the Daishonin's Buddhism as the three martyrs of Atsuhara, and this incident is known as the Atsuhara Persecution.

Having seen that ordinary people would risk their lives for the sake of Buddhism, the Daishonin felt that the time had come to fulfill the purpose of his advent. On October 12, 1279, he inscribed "the Dai-Gohonzon bestowed upon the world."

As evidenced by his behavior and achievements as the Daishonin's disciple, Nikko Shonin far surpassed the five senior priests. In light of Nikko Shonin's faith, practice, study, character and leadership, which were tested through numerous persecutions, it was natural for the Daishonin to entrust his teaching to his most outstanding disciple.

After the Daishonin's death, his ashes were interred in a small temple on Mount Minobu, and the six senior priests were to take turns watching over the ashes. But Hakiri Sanenaga, a steward of Minobu, and his family were swayed by the erroneous teachings of the five senior priests, causing Nikko Shonin to severe his ties with the priests and the Hakiri family.

To protect the integrity of the Daishonin's Buddhism and thus establish the foundation for its future, he left Minobu and moved to Fuji at the invitation of Nanjo Tokimitsu. Nikko Shonin states in his "Reply to Lord Hara": "No matter where we may go, it is of utmost importance to carry on the teaching of the sage and establish it in the world. Although I think in this way, all other disciples have committed treachery against the teacher. Nikko alone knows the correct teaching of the original teacher and thus achieves the true purpose of his life. So I shall never become oblivious to the true intent [of Nichiren]" (*Hennentai Nichiren Daishonin Gosho*, p. 1733).

Stressing the importance of rebuking the destroyers of Buddhism, the Daishonin states: "And if there should be eminent priests who keep the precepts and practice religious austerities, and who appear to be spreading the teachings of the Lotus Sutra but are, in fact, subverting them, you should perceive the truth of the matter and reprimand them" (WND, 518). Following the Daishonin's teaching, Nikko Shonin continued to point out the errors of the five senior priests.

As Nikko Shonin taught through his own example, unless we remain vigilant against corruption and reveal injustice whenever it occurs, the Daishonin's Buddhism will eventually be obscured and lost.

Moreover, if we slacken in our efforts to challenge Nichiren Shoshu's affront on the Daishonin's Buddhism and develop a halfhearted attitude toward slander of the Law, we will eventually destroy our faith and thus the good fortune that we have otherwise accumulated.

As the Daishonin teaches, "It is the way of a devil to assume the form of a venerable monk or to take possession of one's father, mother, or brother in order to obstruct happiness in one's next life" (WND, 81). The essence of the current problem with the Nichiren Shoshu priesthood becomes clear as day when viewed in light of this passage.

In the spring of 1289, nearly seven years after the Daishonin's passing, Nikko Shonin departed from Minobu and stayed for a while at the estate of lay priest Yui—his grandfather on his mother's side. He then moved to Ueno (present-day Fujinomiya City, Shizuoka Prefecture) at the earnest request of Nanjo Tokimitsu, the steward of the area.

Nikko Shonin's Establishment of Taiseki-ji

In October of the following year, Nikko Shonin founded Taiseki-ji on the scenic field of Oishigahara on the Nanjo family's estate. A lodging temple, called Dai-bo or Mutsu-bo, was built for Nikko Shonin. In the area surrounding Dai-bo, other lodging temples were built for Nikko Shonin's disciples: Renzo-bo for Nichimoku, Jakunichi-bo for Nikke, Rikyo-bo for Nisshu, Joren-bo for Nichido, Minamino-bo for Nichizen, Hyakkan-bo for Nissen, Ryosho-bo for Nichijo, and Kujo-bo for Nichizon. At this time, Nikko Shonin also designated his "six main disciples" to preserve the Daisho-nin's Buddhism: they were Nichimoku, Nikke, Nisshu, Nichizen, Nissen and Nichijo ("On the Matters That the Be-lievers of the Fuji School Must Know," GZ, 1603).

On February 15, 1298, Nikko Shonin established a temple to enshrine the Daishonin's image in Omosu, the area adja-cent to Ueno, at the request of its steward Ishikawa Mago-saburo Yoshitada. He then entrusted Nichimoku with Taiseki-ji and moved to Omosu. Nikko Shonin focused on the further education and development of his disciples, who com-muted there to receive instructions from their teacher. This temple in Omosu became known as Omosu Seminary.

At Omosu Seminary, Nikko Shonin read and gave lec-tures on the Daishonin's writings, which he called "Gosho," meaning "the Buddha's writings" ("On the Matters That the Believers of the Fuji School Must Know," GZ, 1604). [The word *gosho* consists of two characters: *go* and *sho*. *Go* is an honorific prefix, meaning "respectable or noble," and *sho* lit-erally means "writings."] Out of the Daishonin's six senior disciples, Nikko Shonin alone understood the importance of these writings. For the sake of posterity, Nikko Shonin copied many of his mentor's writings. Of those, forty-nine copies of the Daishonin's writings are extant today, includ-ing "On Chanting the Daimoku of the Lotus Sutra," "On Establishing the Correct Teaching for the Peace of the Land," excerpts from "The Opening of the Eyes," "The Ob-ject of Devotion for Observing the Mind Established in the Fifth Five-Hundred-Year Period after the Thus Come One's Passing" and "The Essentials of the Lotus Sutra." Besides those copies made by Nikko Shonin, there are only three copies by Nichimoku and two by Nippo still in existence. None of the five senior priests attempted to preserve their teacher's writings.

Furthermore, Nikko Shonin selected the ten major writings of the Daishonin and recorded the location of each of these writings for the sake of future believers. The ten major writings designated by Nikko Shonin are: 1) "On Chanting the Daimoku of the Lotus Sutra"; 2) "On Establishing the Correct Teaching for the Peace of the Land"; 3) "The Opening of the Eyes"; 4) "The Object of Devotion for Observing the Mind"; 5) "The Essentials of the Lotus Sutra"; 6) "The Selection of the Time"; 7) "On Repaying Debts of Gratitude"; 8) "On the Four Stages of Faith and the Five Stages of Practice"; 9) "Letter to Shimoyama"; and 10) "Questions and Answers about Embracing the Lotus Sutra." He selected these writings as essential for the practitioners of the Daishonin's Buddhism and added to the manuscripts the phrase *the essential teaching of the Lotus Sutra.*

Nikko Shonin dedicated his later years to the development of his disciples at Omosu Seminary. According to legend, he expelled a disciple named Nichizon during a lecture for absent-mindedly staring at the leaves falling from a pear tree in the yard, saying: "One who wishes to spread the great Law does not let his mind wander and stare at leaves falling while listening to the preaching of Buddhism" (*Essential Writings of the Fuji School*, vol. 5, p. 227). Spurred by his teacher's strict rebuke, Nichizon traveled throughout various provinces and spread the Daishonin's Buddhism. It is said that after establishing thirty-six temples in twelve years, he was pardoned by his teacher. This story tells us something of Nikko Shonin's dedication to the Daishonin's Buddhism.

A believer named Jakusen-bo Nitcho, originally a disciple of Niko (one of the five senior priests who betrayed the Daishonin), later renounced Niko and chose Nikko Shonin as his mentor. Nikko Shonin appointed Nitcho as the first chief priest of Omosu Seminary, entrusting him with the instruction of student priests. When Nitcho died at a young age, Nikko Shonin appointed Sanmi Nichijun as the second chief priest.

Nichijun wrote: "I received instructions [from Nikko Shonin] at Dai-bo lodging in the morning and, in the evening, preached at Mie-do [where the image of Nichiren Daishonin is enshrined]" (*Essential Writings of the Fuji School*, vol. 2, p. 124). As he states, Nichijun lectured on the Daishonin's writings, such as "The Opening of the Eyes" and "The Object of Devotion for Observing the Mind." In this manner, many young student priests were nurtured, including six new disciples designated by Nikko Shonin: Nichidai, Nitcho, Nichido, Nichimyo, Nichigo and Nichijo.

Meanwhile, Nichimoku stayed at Taiseki-ji. He often visited the estate of his Niida clan and founded several temples and also traveled to many other areas, spreading the Daishonin's Buddhism and developing many new disciples. Furthermore, on behalf of Nikko Shonin, Nichimoku remonstrated with the sovereign forty-two times, visiting the shogunate government in Kamakura and the imperial palace in Kyoto.

During his youth, Nichimoku began traveling so extensively on foot that he seriously injured his left ankle. But this did not prevent him from traveling for the sake of the Daishonin's Buddhism.

When at Taiseki-ji, he led a simple life, which included growing vegetables in the fields. Nichimoku often sent his homegrown melons to Nikko Shonin at Omosu. In one reply, Nikko Shonin writes: "Since I could not harvest melons in my field at Omosu due to the drought, I am grateful for your rare gift" (*One Hundred Sacred Admonitions*, p. 192).

This indicates that Nikko Shonin also lived a modest life, farming himself.

Regarding the behavior and lifestyle of a priest, the Daishonin states: "Priests in the Latter Day of the Law are ignorant of the principles of Buddhism and are conceited, so they despise the correct teacher and fawn on patrons. True priests are those who are honest and who desire little and yet know satisfaction" (WND, 747).

Nikko Shonin and Nichimoku lived in accord with their teacher's expectations while the five senior priests degenerated into "priests in the Latter Day of the Law." The Daishonin severely condemns this type of priest, referring to him as "an animal dressed in priestly robes" (WND, 760).

Nikko Shonin wrote "On the Matters That the Believers of the Fuji School Must Know" (GZ, 1601–09) and "Refuting the Five Senior Priests" (GZ, 1610–16) to clarify the doctrinal differences between himself and the five senior priests. Furthermore, to prevent the destruction of the Daishonin's Buddhism by corrupt priests, Nikko Shonin penned "Twenty-six Admonitions" (GZ, 1617–19) on January 13, 1333.

The Twenty-six Admonitions

In these cautionary articles, Nikko Shonin clarifies that the Fuji School (i.e., the school founded by Nikko Shonin) is the orthodox school of Nichiren Daishonin's Buddhism, while the schools founded by the five senior priests deviate from his mentor's teaching. Nikko Shonin urges his disciples: "Until kosen-rufu is achieved, propagate the Law to the full extent of your ability without begrudging your life" (GZ, 1618). He also teaches his disciples to give their utmost respect to those who practice in accord with the Daishonin's writings.

Nikko Shonin cautions that those priests who seek worldly fame and profit without spreading Buddhism and rebuking slander may not be known as his disciples. Furthermore, he strictly admonishes that even the chief priest of Taiseki-ji (i.e., the high priest of the Fuji School) is not an exception to his warning articles, stating: "Do not follow even the high priest if he goes against the Buddha's Law and propounds his own views" (GZ, 1618).

Throughout his "Twenty-six Admonitions," Nikko Shonin emphasizes that to protect and spread the Daishonin's Buddhism is of utmost importance. Nikko Shonin's fundamental stance may be summarized thusly: Those who wish to practice the Daishonin's Buddhism must regard the Gohonzon and his writings as the bases of faith, and practice and strive toward the widespread propagation of their mentor's teaching. He concludes his admonitions by saying: "Those who violate even one of these articles cannot be called disciples of Nikko" (GZ, 1619).

When we examine the aberrant behavior of the Nichiren Shoshu priesthood in light of Nikko Shonin's "Twenty-six Admonitions," it becomes clear that the SGI is the only group carrying on the orthodoxy of the Daishonin's Buddhism today. Shortly after World War II, Nichiko Hori, the fifty-ninth high priest, said to one of his disciples: "Does the current priesthood have anything other than the Gakkai? The priesthood must be detested if it excludes the Gakkai." But now that it has unilaterally severed its ties with the SGI, Nichiren Shoshu has strayed from the Daishonin's Buddhism.

On February 7, 1333, soon after completing "Twenty-six Admonitions," Nikko Shonin died at Omosu, at age eighty-eight. Before his passing, Nikko Shonin appointed

Nichimoku as his successor in a document titled "Articles Regarding the Succession of Nikko," dated November 10, 1330 (*EssentialWritings of the Fuji School*, vol. 8, p. 17).

Until his death, Nikko Shonin continued to lead the spread of the Daishonin's Buddhism, responding to the expectations placed on him by his mentor, who referred to him as "the great leader of the propagation of true Buddhism" (GZ, 1600). Under Nikko Shonin's leadership, Nichimoku and other disciples also made valiant efforts in propagation. As a result, by the time of Nikko Shonin's death, the Fuji School had spread throughout Japan—from Tohoku, the northeastern part of Japan's main island (present-day Miyagi, Yamagata and Fukushima prefectures) down to the southern island of Kyushu (present-day Fukuoka and Miyazaki prefectures).

Because Nikko Shonin spread the Daishonin's Buddhism despite persecution and protected its integrity when threatened by the five senior priests, he is regarded as the treasure of the *samgha* or group of believers—priests and lay believers alike—dedicated to the transmission and preservation of the Buddha's teaching. The *samgha* has been regarded as one of the three treasures of Buddhism along with the treasures of the Buddha and the Law (i.e., the Buddha's teaching) because, without it, people could not possibly benefit from the treasures of the Buddha and the Law. As Buddhism migrated from India to China and then to Japan, the functions of the *samgha* were fulfilled chiefly by the clergy. Hence the *samgha* came to denote the Buddhist priesthood, and thus the treasure of the *samgha* has often been translated as the treasure of the priesthood.

In the Fuji School, the treasure of the Buddha is Nichiren Daishonin because he expounded the Mystic Law, which enables all people to reveal their innate Buddhahood; the treasure of the Law is the Gohonzon bestowed upon all humanity because it is the essence of the Daishonin's teaching; and the treasure of the *samgha* is Nikko Shonin because, as mentioned previously, he correctly transmitted and preserved the Daishonin's Buddhism. Without his efforts, we could not enjoy the benefit of the Daishonin's Buddhism today.

Regarding the three treasures of the Fuji School, Nittatsu Hosoi, the sixty-sixth high priest, stated:

> In our school, the three treasures are established as follows: the treasure of the Law is the Gohonzon; the treasure of the Buddha is the Daishonin; and the treasure of the *samgha* is Nikko Shonin. . . . The successive high priests are not the same as the Daishonin. The high priest is often described falsely as the Daishonin himself, and this causes problems. I wish to clarify this point." (From a sermon delivered on May 26, 1977)

The current Nichiren Shoshu priesthood, however, propounds that "the high priest is the Daishonin of the modern day" (June 1991 *Dai-Nichiren*) and that "the high priest and the Dai-Gohonzon are one and inseparable" (a document by the Nichiren Shoshu executive priests dated September 6, 1991). These assertions clearly ignore the meaning of the three treasures in the Daishonin's Buddhism.

Regarding believers' reverence for the three treasures, Nittatsu Hosoi also stated: "In short, the correct way of our school is to regard the Gohonzon of the oneness of the Person and the Law as the basis of all. In the Gohonzon are contained all of the three treasures. When you enshrine the Gohonzon in a Buddhist altar and exert yourself in faith

morning and evening, you are already paying sufficient respect toward the three treasures" (from a sermon delivered
on July 27, 1977). In other words, to revere the three treasures
of the Daishonin's Buddhism means to regard the Gohonzon as the basis of faith and practice.

The current priesthood's erroneous interpretation of the
three treasures clearly indicates its ignorance of the Daishonin's Buddhism as well as of Nikko Shonin's efforts to
spread and protect his mentor's teaching.

CHAPTER 3

The Schism
After Nichimoku

On May 22, 1333, a few months after Nikko Shonin's passing, the army of Nitta Yoshisada defeated the ruling Hojo clan, bringing an end to the Kamakura shogunate. When Emperor Godaigo reestablished the imperial government in Kyoto, Nikko's successor, Nichimoku, felt that it was an opportune time to remonstrate with the sovereign and proclaim the validity of the Daishonin's Buddhism. So, at the beginning of November, Nichimoku, accompanied by two of his disciples—Nichizon and Nichigo—went to Kyoto.

A Seventy-Two-Year Land Dispute

He wasn't content to live quietly at Taiseki-ji but, following the spirit of this teacher, actively devoted himself to propagating the Daishonin's teachings, traveling far and wide to do so.

On his way to the nation's new political center, however, Nichimoku collapsed—probably due both to age and exhaustion from cold weather—at Tarui, Mino Province. On November 15, he died at age seventy-four, bringing closure to a life dedicated to the spread of the Daishonin's Buddhism.

Nichigo returned to Fuji with Nichimoku's ashes. Nichizon went on to Kyoto and waited for an opportunity to remonstrate with the government.

Before his passing, Nichimoku designated Nichigo as the chief priest of Renzo-bo, a lodging temple on the grounds of Taiseki-ji. But Nichigo later had a dispute over doctrine with Nichido, the fourth high priest (*Essential Writings of the Fuji School*, vol. 9, p. 36). Eventually his arguments were rejected by the majority of priests at Taiseki-ji, and he was forced to leave for Awa Province where he had once been sent to propagate the Daishonin's teaching.

Nichigo felt a strong sense of rivalry with Nichido. It is said that when Nichimoku left for Kyoto to remonstrate with the imperial government, he unofficially designated Nichido as his successor (*Detailed Accounts of Nikko Shonin of the Fuji School*, p. 478). Since Nichimoku had to retain his position as high priest to represent the Fuji School in remonstrating with the imperial government, his transfer of the office of high priest to Nichido was conducted privately. After the private appointment, Nichido moved into Dai-bo, the lodging temple for the high priest, and assumed administrative responsibilities for Taiseki-ji.

To attain superiority over Nichido, Nichigo schemed to obtain control of the property around Renzo-bo of Taiseki-ji from Nanjo Tokitsuna, the steward of the area and head of the Nanjo family. As the fifth son of Nanjo Tokimitsu, the donor of Taiseki-ji's property, Tokitsuna had great influence over the management of Taiseki-ji. Concerned with status and wealth, Nichigo asserted his property right against Nichido and, in so doing, violated the intent of Nikko Shonin, who declared: "Those of insufficient learning who are bent on obtaining fame and fortune are not qualified to call themselves my followers" (GZ, 1618).

All of Taiseki-ji's land had been donated by Nanjo Toki-mitsu to Nikko Shonin. Nanjo Tokitsuna, however, wrote up a new deed for the east side of Taiseki-ji's property and transferred it to Nichigo on the condition that Tokitsuna's second son, Go'omaru, who was still very young at the time, become Nichigo's successor. The son would later be known as Nichiden.

Based on the deed from Nanjo Tokitsuna, Nichigo lodged a complaint with the governor of Suruga Province. The provincial government acknowledged Nichigo's right for the time being, and he returned to Renzo-bo at Taiseki-ji and built a hall nearby to enshrine the Daishonin's image. Nichigo also schemed to gain the support of the priests at Omosu Semi-nary, vigorously asserting his authority over Nichido.

Nichigo, however, met with strong resistance from many priests and was once again forced to leave Taiseki-ji. When Nichigo left, he took a statue of the Daishonin and a Gohon-zon inscribed by the Daishonin. He moved to Awa Province and established Myohon-ji at Hota. He also built a seminary at Koizumi near Ueno where Taiseki-ji was located. This seminary later became known as Kuon-ji.

Nichigo died in 1353, but for more than seventy years his followers continued to argue for control of the eastern por-tion of Taiseki-ji. Nanjo Tokitsuna's son Nichiden, by then the second chief priest of Myohon-ji, filed a suit with the Imagawa family, the ruling clan of Suruga Province, and eventually regained control of the property.

Taiseki-ji, headed by Nichiji, the sixth high priest, ap-pealed the decision to the more powerful Uesugi family of the Kanto region, which included Suruga Province. At last, the governor of the Kanto region ordered the governor of Suruga

Province to transfer the deed for the eastern part of Taiseki-ji to its original owner—Taiseki-ji. When Nichiden died in 1416 at age seventy-seven, this long dispute effectively ended. Nichiden's entire life was spent on this land dispute.

The seventy-two-yearlong land dispute, born out of Nichigo's greed for status and wealth, resulted in Taiseki-ji's considerable decline and impeded the further spread of the Daishonin's Buddhism.

After Nichimoku's passing in 1333, Nichizon continued his trip to Kyoto. It is said that in the following year, he had an audience with the imperial government and received a piece of property in the nation's capital where he established Jogyo-in temple.

Nichizon Establishes Shakyamuni's Statue as an Object of Devotion

Nichizon is known for having been expelled from Omosu Seminary by Nikko Shonin for vacantly staring at falling leaves during a sermon (see chapter 2 for more explanation). Nichizon took faith in the Daishonin's Buddhism under the tutelage of Nichimoku. Formerly a Tendai priest, however, he could not correctly grasp the Daishonin's teaching that people's disregard of the Lotus Sutra and their faith in lesser teachings cause the Buddhist deities (the positive functions of life and the universe) to abandon the land, thus inviting disaster. There are reports that he performed an "eye-opening ceremony" on a statue of Amida Buddha as well as Bodhisattva Jizo (Skt Kshitigarbha). Nichizon also enshrined Shakyamuni's statue and the statues of his ten major disciples as objects of worship. This demonstrates that Nichizon misunderstood the Daishonin's Buddhism and went against the intent of Nikko Shonin. Because the branch school derived from Nichizon advocated the recitation of the entire Lotus Sutra and the worship of Shakyamuni's statue, it gradually distanced itself from Taiseki-ji.

Nichidai, one of Nichizon's disciples, founded Juhon-ji in Kyoto. When Juhon-ji and Jogyo-in were burned down by the priests of Enryaku-ji in 1550, Juhon-ji chief priest Nisshin combined the two temples and established Yobo-ji (also pronounced as Yoho-ji).

Nichigo and Nichizon, who accompanied Nichimoku on his last trip to remonstrate with the government, strayed from the Daishonin's Buddhism because of their desire for status and wealth and their shallow knowledge of Buddhism. Soon after the deaths of Nikko Shonin and Nichimoku in 1333, a little more than fifty years after the Daishonin's death, the Fuji School already gave rise to two unorthodox off-shoots—one from Nichigo and another from Nichizon. Because of their distortion of the Daishonin's Buddhism, the Fuji School declined significantly and lost its momentum in spreading the Daishonin's Buddhism.

Furthermore, on January 7, 1334, at Joren-bo (also known as Hyakkan-bo) on the grounds of Taiseki-ji, Nissen, one of Nikko Shonin's six main disciples, and Nichidai, one of Nikko Shonin's six new disciples, debated whether a practitioner should recite the "Expedient Means" chapter of the Lotus Sutra as part of the Buddhist practice.

Nichidai, who was a nephew of Nikko Shonin, had studied at Omosu Seminary. Nikko Shonin appointed him as chief priest of the seminary although he was young. In his debate with Nissen, Nichidai asserted that one could benefit from the "Expedient Means" chapter, which is from the theoretical first half of the Lotus Sutra. But the priests at the seminary criticized Nichidai for his position, and the steward of the area also did not support him. So, although he was the chief priest, he was forced to leave Omosu Seminary (which later became known as Kitayama Honmon-ji) and move to Nishiyama. There he established Hokke-do (which later became known as Nishiyama Honmon-ji). With the expulsion of Nichidai, Nishiyama Honmon-ji and Kitayama Honmon-ji vigorously fought each other over the orthodoxy inherited from Nikko Shonin.

CHAPTER 4

High-Ranking Priests Sell Off Taiseki-ji

As a result of its seventy-two–yearlong land dispute with Nichigo and his followers, Taiseki-ji declined considerably (see chapter 3 for more information).

Nichiu's Restoration of the Sect

The dispute exhausted the head temple's financial and human resources. The number of student priests studying at the temple decreased, and the temple lost many branch temples due to the internal turmoil. There is an account of Nichiei, the eighth high priest (1352–1419), transferring the heritage of the Law to a lay believer as its temporary keeper because of a lack of capable priests at Taiseki-ji. "The Accounts of the Fuji School" states: "High Priest Nichiei commented to other priests: 'It is my sadness and lament that there is no opportunity to transmit the heritage of the Law.' At last, in the twenty-sixth year of O'ei [1419], when he fell ill, he bestowed the heritage of the Law upon Aburano Joren" (*Essential Writings of the Fuji School*, vol. 5, p. 255).

If this account is true, the ninth high priest, Nichiu (1402–82), presumably received the transmission from the lay person Aburano Joren at age seventeen. He was from the respected Nanjo family and became known as a restorer of the Fuji School because he contributed to the maintenance and repair of buildings at the head temple, the development of student priests and the restoration of branch temples. Nichiu's scholarship was also well known, and many student priests visited him at Taiseki-ji.

While managing Taiseki-ji, Nichiu traveled extensively to spread the Daishonin's Buddhism. He went east to Oshu, the northeastern region of Japan's main island, and west to Kyoto, the seat of the imperial government. He also visited Echigo Province in the north and further on to Sado Island. In 1432, he submitted a letter of remonstration to the Ashikaga shogunate government in Kyoto. Many of the old temples of the Fuji School in the northeastern region of the main island are said to have been founded by Nichiu.

"The Accounts of Teacher Nichiu," compiled by Nichi'in, the thirty-first high priest, recounts this incident: Once while Nichiu was away from Taiseki-ji, the three high-ranking priests appointed by him to protect Taiseki-ji during his absence changed the ownership of the head temple and sold it off:

> [Teacher Nichiu] appointed three priests as his deputies during his absence. But who knows what they had in mind? These deputies abandoned this temple [Taiseki-ji], so for six years, it was a place slanderous of the Law. But when the elder priest [Nichiu] returned, he restored the spirit of the sage, the respectable founder [Nichiren Daishonin]. Although it had become a place of slander, he purchased Taiseki-ji back from Lord Okutsu for twenty *kan* of coins, thereby restoring the spirit of the sage, the respectable

founder. (*Essential Writings of the Fuji School*, vol. 1, pp. 185–86)

Regarding this incident, Nichiko Hori, the fifty-ninth high priest and noted authority of the history of the Fuji School, comments:

> Put simply, he [High Priest Nichiu] appointed three deputies. But the three of them sold off Taiseki-ji according to other documents. Then High Priest Nichiu, it is recorded, returned and banished them. Those three or four deputies were all high-ranking priests because they had the title of *ajari*. . . . We do not know who purchased it [Taiseki-ji] or under whose name it was registered. Probably the deputies changed the ownership to their own names. If someone respectable had bought it, I do not think that he would have given it up so easily. So I think that the deputies changed the ownership into their names. (From "On the History of the Fuji School: An Interview With High Priest Nichiko," November 1956 *The Daibyakurenge*)

This incident attests to the condition of the priesthood during the late fifteenth century. While Nichiu was traveling far and wide to spread the Daishonin's teachings, corrupt high-ranking priests at Taiseki-ji were concerned only about their interests. Dealing with the corruption within his own priesthood is another reason Nichiu is known as a restorer of the Fuji School.

To fight the spiritual decay in the priesthood, Nichiu strictly reminded his disciples of the Daishonin's earnest desire to

**Nichiu Attempts
To Restore the
Daishonin's Spirit**

spread his teachings, stating:

According to the words of the respectable founder [Nichiren Daishonin], we should continue to spread [the Law] widely even under stupas or bridges so long as the king and his subjects do not take faith in it. We should not be idle in our dwellings even for a moment. We should not be seeking wealth nor high status. (*Essential Writings of the Fuji School*, vol. 1, p. 208)

He also writes:

Since our age is already into the Latter Day of the Law, this school, influenced by the conditions of society, entered the Latter Day as well. This is because our faith has become weaker than in the past. Furthermore, we have become extremely lax in terms of rebuking the sins of slandering the Law. In short, I think, now is the Latter Day of this school, which I find most difficult. (*Essential Writings of the Fuji School*, vol. 2, pp. 139–40)

Nichiu's statement indicates that about a hundred years after Nikko Shonin's death, priests' faith and spirit to preserve the integrity of the Daishonin's teaching had already weakened considerably. In his attempt to revive the Daishonin's teaching, Nichiu exerted himself in propagation and study. Despite his efforts, however, many priests lost faith and became corrupt.

The Daishonin himself was a reformer who revived faith in the Lotus Sutra. Because he realized that the Lotus Sutra was the correct teaching for the time, he was especially strict toward the Tendai sect, which claimed to be an orthodox school of the Lotus Sutra while distorting its teachings and compromising with Shingon esotericism. The Daishonin criticized the Tendai sect more than two hundred times in about sixty writings. In his criticism of the Tendai sect, he did not mince words, referring to the sect as "a thief of the Law" (GZ, 1004), "the foremost slanderers of the Law" (GZ, 1067) and "the beginning of our country's ruin" (WND, 812). He condemns priests Jikaku, Annen and Eshin of the Tendai sect by describing them as "the three worms who devoured the lion-body of the Lotus Sutra and the Great Teacher Dengyo" (WND, 578).

The reformist spirit to revive the humanistic ideals of the Lotus Sutra is at the core of the Daishonin's Buddhism. Unless this commitment is widely shared among believers, the stream of his teaching will become corrupt and eventually run dry as demonstrated by the history of Taiseki-ji.

Nanjo Nichiju, one of Nichiu's disciples, compiled many of Nichiu's instructions on the teachings and traditions of the Fuji School in "On the Formalities of True Buddhism." In this writing, Nichiu confirms some of the fundamental aspects of the Daishonin's teaching. For example, he states: "The object of devotion in this school shall be limited to that of Sage Nichiren" (*Essential Writings of the Fuji School*, vol. 1, p. 65). He also states: "In the Hokke [Lotus] sect [i.e., the Fuji

Nichiu's Understanding of the Heritage of the Law

School], we must not regard [the images] of the Buddhas and the bodhisattvas such as Kannon [Skt Avalokiteshvara] or Myoon [Skt Gadgadasvara] as objects of devotion no matter how artfully they are painted. We shall make use only of the object of devotion in which Sage Nichiren inscribed the Ten Worlds" (*Essential Writings of the Fuji School*, vol. 1, p. 70). These statements by Nichiu suggest that there was confusion about the object of worship within the Fuji School.

Regarding the concept of the heritage of the Law, Nichiu states:

> Faith, the heritage of the Law and the pure flow of the Law are identical. Continuous faith indicates the unbroken lineage and thus the correctly transmitted heritage of the Law and the uninterrupted pure flow of the Law. As a person shall not contradict his or her parents in the secular world, we in the religious world shall not go astray from what is in the heart of our teacher in order to receive the correct heritage and pure flow of the Law. When our faith does not differ from that of the noble founder, our body and mind manifest as the body and mind of Myoho-renge-kyo. When our faith differs [from that of the noble founder], however, we are ordinary mortals in body and mind. Then we do not possess the heritage of the Law that allows us to attain Buddhahood in our present forms. (*Essential Writings of the Fuji School*, vol. 1, p. 64)

The Japanese term for the heritage of the Law is *kechimyaku*, which literally means "bloodstream," indicating how a Buddhist teaching is transmitted flawlessly from teacher to disciple just as blood flows in the human body.

Nichiko Hori, the fifty-ninth high priest and noted Buddhist scholar, comments on the above passage by Nichiu:

> When we do not go astray in the slightest from the faith of the great teachers of Buddhism, that is, Great Sage Nichiren, the noble founder, and Nikko Shonin, the founder [of Taiseki-ji], we as their followers shall transform our evil and defiled minds into the body and mind of Myoho-renge-kyo, which is true, good and pure. Such a transformation of body and mind depends upon sincere faith and earnest practice. If we do not reverently uphold these essentials, our faith becomes unsound, impure, evil and confused, thus contradicting the Buddha's intent. Then we will obstruct the passage of the pure flow of the Law, so we will manifest our intrinsic self as deluded ordinary mortals in body and mind. Thus we will destroy our qualification to inherit the heritage of the Law that allows us to attain Buddhahood in our present form. This is unfortunate. (*Essential Writings of the Fuji School*, vol. 1, p. 176)

It is through faith as taught by the Daishonin that we receive the heritage of the Law and reveal ourselves as entities of the Mystic Law, as Buddhas.

The lifeline of the Daishonin's Buddhism lies in faith. If believers lose faith, there can be no prospect for their enlightenment. Even the high priest will not receive the heritage of the Law if he loses faith. As high priest, his betrayal of people's trust and expectations in his office becomes a function of what Buddhism terms "the devil king of the sixth heaven," or the negative workings that obscure one's innate

Buddhahood. Quoting from the Nirvana Sutra, the Daisho-nin refers to those who assume a saintly appearance yet obstruct the spread of the Lotus Sutra after the Buddha's passing as "devils in the guise of a Buddha" (GZ, 76). As the Daishonin cautions us, we must be aware of such negative potential lurking in religious authority.

If the heritage of the Law is faith, something shared by all believers, then what does the priesthood's interpretation of the transmission of the heritage of the Law from one high priest to another mean? We can see the prototype of this transmission in the transfer of the office of high priest from Nikko Shonin to the third high priest, Nichimoku. The following is the entire translation of the document titled "Articles Regarding the Succession of Nikko" (Jpn *Nikko Ato Jojo no Koto*) dated November 10, 1330:

> When Honmon-ji [the Temple of True Buddhism] is built, Niidakyo Ajari Nichimoku shall become its chief priest. In Japan and the rest of the entire world, half the temples shall be administered by Nichimoku's successors, and the other half by other priests.
>
> Nikko shall bestow upon Nichimoku the Dai-Go-honzon inscribed in the second year of Koan [1279] as well as the documents drawn up in the fifth year of Koan [1282].
>
> Nichimoku shall conduct gongyo and await the time of kosen-rufu while administering and repairing the temple at Oishi [Taiseki-ji] — both its halls and cemetery. The aforementioned Nichimoku, at the age of fifteen, met Nikko and took faith in the Lotus Sutra. Since then until now at age seventy-three, he has not committed an error. At the age of seventeen,

he visited Sage Nichiren's dwelling at Mount Minobu in Kai province and stayed there for seven years constantly at his service. Since his passing, through the eighth year of Koan [1285] till the second year of Gentoku [1330], for fifty years, the merits in his remonstrance with the sovereign have been distinguished from those of others. Thus I set down so that this may serve as proof for posterity. (*Essential Writings of the Fuji School*, vol. 8, p. 18)

From this document it is clear that the transfer of the heritage of the Law from one high priest to another boils down to the transfer of the administrative responsibilities associated with the office. These responsibilities include the management of Taiseki-ji and its branch temples and the safekeeping of the Dai-Gohonzon and some documents. It should also be noted that Nikko Shonin's appointment was not arbitrary. He states in the transfer document that Nichimoku is qualified to be his successor because of his outstanding faith and consistent practice from the age of fifteen to seventy-three. Nichimoku was appointed because of his courage to remonstrate with the sovereign as well as his passion to seek instructions from the Daishonin at Mount Minobu. The transfer document "Articles Regarding the Succession of Nikko" explains that the transfer of the heritage of the Law from one high priest to another is the transfer of the administrative responsibilities of that office, and the essential qualification for the office of high priest lies in faith and practice.

The priesthood explains that Nichimoku "directly inherited the Living Essence from Nikko Shonin" (*The Liturgy of Nichiren Shoshu*, Nichiren Shoshu Head Temple Taiseki-ji edition, English version, p. 35). This "Living Essence," which is also referred to as "the entity of the heritage of the Law," has been passed down from one high priest to another for more than seven hundred years, according to the priesthood. Despite the priesthood's efforts to mystify this "Living Essence" supposedly possessed only by the high priest, Nikko Shonin clearly indicates in his transfer document to Nichimoku that it is nothing other than the Dai-Gohonzon.

In this regard, Nichio, the fifty-sixth high priest, states: "The entity of the Law specifically entrusted [to the successive high priests] is the Dai-Gohonzon of the High Sanctuary of True Buddhism kept in secrecy at our temple" *(Bennaku Kanjin Sho*, p. 212). What the priesthood calls the transfer of "Living Essence" from one high priest to another is essentially the transfer of the high priest's administrative responsibility to protect the Dai-Gohonzon. Needless to say, with this responsibility must come the high priest's faith and practice for the propagation of the Daishonin's Buddhism as Nikko Shonin saw in his successor, Nichimoku.

By describing the transfer of the office of high priest with terms like "the Living Essence of the True Buddha," the priesthood tries to create a myth that there is some secret teaching that only the high priest knows. All the transfer documents from the Daishonin to Nikko Shonin are, in one sense, explanations of the Gohonzon. For example, some documents discuss the Daishonin's Buddhism implicit in the "Life Span" chapter of the Lotus Sutra, and others discuss the doctrinal comparison between the Daishonin's Buddhism and Shakyamuni's Buddhism. These teachings were not widely known nor accepted in the early days of the Fuji School; therefore, they were considered "secret."

However, all the so-called transfer documents or secret

traditions of the Fuji School have already been published. There is no important doctrinal document accessible only by the high priest. Nichiko Hori, the fifty-ninth high priest, who is well known for his scholarship, compiled all the major documents of the Fuji School and published them as the *Complete Works of the Fuji School*. From this work, Nichiko Hori selected important documents and published them as the *Essential Writings of the Fuji School*. In the first volume of this collection, he published the eight transfer documents. Furthermore, in 1952, at the request of President Toda, *Nichiren Daishonin Gosho Zenshu* (The Collected Writings of Nichiren Daishonin) was published under the editorial supervision of Nichiko Hori. This collection of the Daishonin's writings also includes major documents transferred from the Daishonin to Nikko Shonin.

In the eighteenth century, the twenty-sixth high priest, Nichikan, systematized the Daishonin's teachings and made a clear distinction between the Daishonin's Buddhism and that of Shakyamuni in works such as his *Six-volume Writings* and various commentaries. In the past, before the appearance of the Soka Gakkai, Nichikan's writings were also considered "secret traditions" and were next in importance to the transfer documents. Thus they were available only to a handful of people. President Toda, however, in his efforts to promote Buddhist study, made Nichikan's writings available and encouraged people to study them. He said, "In terms of Buddhist study, we must return to the time of High Priest Nichikan."

Ultimately, there is no special significant teaching that only priests know, for the Daishonin makes it clear that there is no secret teaching. To assert that only the high priest knows a certain secret teaching or that only through the high priest can one correctly practice the Daishonin's teaching contradicts the Daishonin's teaching and intent.

As Nittatsu Hosoi, the sixty-sixth high priest, states:

> Nichiren Daishonin's writings are based upon the Lotus Sutra. His writings give life to the sutra and present guidelines for its spread. They open the way for kosen-rufu. The Daishonin appeared in the Latter Day of the Law and revealed himself to be a Buddha. So he is the Buddha of the Latter Day. His teachings are contained in his writings. This is why we must imbue our hearts and minds with the Daishonin's writings. (From a speech delivered on July 27, 1974)

As long as we SGI members continue to develop firm faith in the Gohonzon and practice for kosen-rufu in accord with the Daishonin's writings, the heritage of the Daishonin's Buddhism that enables us to reveal our innate Buddhahood will continue to flow in our lives.

The priesthood likes to emphasize the ceremonial formalities regarding the transfer of the office of high priest. It asserts that "the specific lifeblood of the entity of the Law received by only a single person" has been handed down within the priesthood through "bequeathing the Golden Utterance to the direct successors" (*Refuting the Soka Gakkai's "Counterfeit Object of Worship"—100 Questions and Answers*, compiled by the Nichiren Shoshu Doctrinal Research Committee, p. 24). The records of the Fuji School, however, do not indicate that "bequeathing the Golden Utterance" has been conducted without fail from one high priest to the next throughout its history. For example, in the early seventeenth century, Nichiju, the sixteenth high priest, could not be with

Nissho, the fifteenth high priest, at the time of his death, so the latter transferred the heritage of high priest to his deputy, Rikyobo Nichigi, as a temporary custodian of the heritage. Nichigi later transferred it to Nichiju.

In response to criticism that the transmission was severed because a proper ceremony was not conducted between the two high priests, Nichiko Hori, the fifty-ninth high priest, states:

> The issue may arise regarding whether the trans-
> mission of the lineage of high priest lies in the formal-
> ity of bequeathing the Golden Utterance to the direct
> successors or in the person of the recipient. If the ap-
> propriate authority resides in the recipient, the trans-
> fer ceremony is merely a formality to establish his
> authority, and the case of Teacher Nichiju does not
> present any inconvenience resulting from the sever-
> ance of the lineage or the interruption of the flow of
> the Law. But if the authority [of high priest] derives
> only from the formalities and the recipient may be
> anyone, then the aforementioned case would be an
> unfortunate instance in the secession of the heritage.
> (From "The Rebuttal to and the Historical Examina-
> tion of the Severance of the Lineage of High
> Priest," *Dai-Nichiren*)

The followers of the Fuji School have been told that the lineage of the high priest has been handed down orally from one high priest to the next. If so, however, such a tradition requires that the recipient stay by the current high priest to receive the lineage before he dies. In the past when there was much difficulty with transportation and communication, it was only natural that sometimes the recipient could not do so. In those cases, a third person would receive the lineage of high priest temporarily before transferring it to the next high priest.

As mentioned before, what has been transferred from one high priest to the next (or what the priesthood refers to as "the specific lifeblood of the entity of the Law received by only a single person") is nothing other than the responsibility of safekeeping the Dai-Gohonzon along with other administrative functions. So the transfer ceremony was a formality to make it known among other priests and followers that the transfer of the office of high priest was conducted between the high priest and a certain recipient. If the transfer ceremony were vital to the transmission of some secret oral teachings, then the lineage of high priest and its secret traditions would have become extinct a long time ago.

Besides the case of the fifteenth high priest, Nissho, there are instances where high priests died without conducting a transfer ceremony or appointing a successor: In 1830, Nisso, the forty-ninth high priest; in 1836, Nichijo, the fiftieth high priest. In 1865, following a great fire at Taiseki-ji, Nichijo, the fifty-third high priest, vanished from the head temple without appointing his successor, and his whereabouts were unknown for some time. In those cases, retired high priests are said to have appointed the next high priest. Historical records prove that a "mystical" transfer ceremony of the office of high priest was never an absolute.

Nichiren Daishonin's Buddhism explains that people can reveal their innate Buddhahood by embracing the Gohonzon. In "The Real Aspect of the Gohonzon," the Daishonin writes: "What is most important is that, by chanting Nam-myoho-renge-kyo alone, you can attain Buddhahood"

(WND, 832). The current priesthood describes the simple transfer of the administrative responsibilities of high priest as "the specific lifeblood of the entity of the Law received by only a single person," thereby suggesting that there is a secret teaching known only to the high priest or that only the high priest possesses "the Living Essence of the True Buddha"—as though it were some mysterious spiritual entity. In the Daishonin's Buddhism, however, the heritage of the Law needed to attain Buddhahood lies only in our earnest faith and practice. To say otherwise amounts to the denial of the Daishonin's teaching and intent.

CHAPTER 5

The Doctrine of the High Priest's Infallibility

Nichiu's tenure as the ninth high priest spanned some forty-eight years until he retired and transferred the office to

**Protecting a
Child High Priest**

Nichijo in 1467. Nichiu moved to Sugiyama in Kai province where he had a temple built. In 1470, Nichijo transferred the office to Nittei. However, both Nichijo and Nittei died in 1472, and Nichiu came out of retirement to assume the office of high priest once again.

According to *The Chronology of the Fuji School*, Nichiu transferred the lineage to thirteen-year-old Nitchin, the twelfth high priest, in 1482, but the exact date is unknown (vol. 1, p. 87). In 1526, Nitchin, known as the "child high priest," appointed eight-year-old Nichiin as his successor. The following year Nitchin died, and Nichiin became the thirteenth high priest at nine.

In fifteenth- and sixteenth-century Japan, feudal lords often inherited their family estates when they were very young, and family stewards were entrusted with their education and care until they were old enough to assume the administrative responsibilities. Following this secular custom, the priesthood at Taiseki-ji began appointing the children of powerful feudal lords as successors to the office of high priest. This indicates both the shortage of capable candidates and the influence of family lineage.

Many priests and members of the head temple's parish expressed deep concern about the ability of these children, especially in their understanding of Buddhist doctrine. When Nitchin became high priest at thirteen, his patron priest, Sakyo Nikkyo, propounded a new doctrine to silence this criticism—the infallibility of the high priest. Sakyo Nikkyo writes: "To have an audience with the high priest, who is a reincarnation of the Sage [Nichiren], is to meet and form a relationship with the living Sage [Nichiren]" (*Essential Writings of the Fuji School*, vol. 2, p. 309); "When those who embrace the [Lotus] Sutra have an audience with the current high priest, they meet with the original Buddha" (ibid., vol. 2, p. 329); and "Each successive high priest who received the transmission of the heritage of the Law is the Gohonzon as Sage Nichiren" (ibid., vol. 4, p. 29).

Sakyo Nikkyo equated the Daishonin with the current high priest by linking the two through the erroneous notion of the transmission of the heritage of the Law. Simply put, Sakyo Nikkyo invoked the Daishonin's name to deify the high priest, but he cites no doctrinal basis from the Daishonin's writings. In the history of the Fuji School, the concept of the high priest's infallibility was put forth only when his ability and authority were in question and needed support.

According to records kept by Nichiji, the sixth high priest, Nikko Shonin is said to have stated that if he grows old and senile and starts invoking the name of Amida Buddha, he must be abandoned (*The Record of Taiseki-ji*). Nikko Shonin also states: "Do not follow even the high priest if he goes against the Buddha's Law and propounds his own views" (GZ, 1618). It was with full awareness of the possibility of an aberrant high priest that Nikko Shonin made these statements. He clearly did not espouse the doctrine of the high priest's infallibility. Furthermore, the host of misguided high priests in the history of the Fuji School refutes such an idea.

Some of the most important transfer documents that the Daishonin wrote to Nikko Shonin were lost in the late sixteenth century due to a feud between two offshoot branches of the Fuji School: the Kitayama Honmon-ji school and the Nishiyama Honmon-ji school. Both temples used the name *Honmon-ji*—"temple of the true teaching"—the name that was said to be assumed by the temple upholding the Daishonin's teachings at the time of kosen-rufu.

Transfer Documents Lost in Feud

Kitayama Honmon-ji derived from Omosu Seminary, which was founded by Nikko Shonin. Nichidai had been appointed as the chief priest of the seminary, but he was later rejected by the seminary priests and forced to leave his post. After Nichidai left, Nichimyo became the chief priest of Omosu Seminary, which gradually distanced itself from Taiseki-ji and renamed itself Kitayama Honmon-ji.

After his ouster, Nichidai eventually moved to Nishiyama and had a temple built there. In reaction to Omosu Seminary taking on the name Honmon-ji, Nichidai named his temple Nishiyama Honmon-ji and continued to assert its orthodoxy over Kitayama Honmon-ji through Nichidai's connection to Nikko Shonin.

These two branches of the Fuji School, which evolved out of Nikko Shonin's Omosu Seminary, carried on an intense rivalry. The Nishiyama school even filed suit against the Kitayama school to reclaim control of the seminary and the Daishonin's statue that was kept there.

On March 17, 1581, some priests from Nishiyama, escorted by some one hundred soldiers, went to Kitayama and took its "treasure box." This box was said to contain many Gohonzon inscribed by the Daishonin, some originals of the Daishonin's writings such as "On the Three Great Secret Laws" as well as some transfer documents, including the two transfer documents in which Nichiren Daishonin entrusted Nikko Shonin as his successor. Other works believed to have been in the treasure box include: "On the Birth of the Original Buddha"; "Seven Articles on the Object of Worship"; "One-hundred-and-six Comparisons"; and "On the Buddhism of the True Cause."

According to one record, Nisshun, the chief priest of Nishiyama Honmon-ji, lodged a suit with Takeda Katsuyori and obtained permission to search Kitayama. Nisshun went to Kitayama and demanded to inspect the contents of its treasure box, claiming that some important treasures had recently been lost from Kuon-ji, a temple at Mount Minobu. When Nichiden, Kitayama chief priest, reluctantly brought out the box, Nisshun took it back to the estate of the Takeda clan in Kai province, claiming that the contents would need further investigation (*Essential Writings of the Fuji School*, vol. 9, p. 22).

Nichiden immediately went to Kofu, the seat of the Kai provincial government, and demanded that the Takeda clan return Kitayama's property. His appeal, however, fell on deaf ears. In protest Nichiden went on a hunger strike and died in

February 1582. The following month, however, the forces of the neighboring lord, Oda Nobunaga, defeated Takeda Katsuyori's army. During the confusion surrounding Takeda's defeat, many of the items in Kitayama's treasure box were lost.

Honda Sakuzaemon, a retainer of Tokugawa Ieyasu, the founder of the Tokugawa shogunate government, later recovered some of the lost items and donated them to Nishiyama. Nisshutsu, the chief priest of Kitayama, lodged a complaint with Tokugawa Ieyasu to reclaim its lost property. Acknowledging the merit of Nisshutsu's complaint, Tokugawa Ieyasu ordered the return of the remaining sixty-four items to Kitayama.

Due to this incident, many important documents and Gohonzon inscribed by the Daishonin were lost. Some scholars later denied the Daishonin's transfer of his lineage to Nikko Shonin, claiming that the two transfer documents and "On the Three Great Secret Laws" were forged. But copies that had been made before the loss of the originals still existed, and the background of the incident, which resulted in the loss of the originals, was documented. Thus their refutation of Nikko Shonin's legitimacy could not be substantiated.

CHAPTER 6

The Parish System and the Rise of Funeral Buddhism

In 1336, Nichizon, a disciple of Nikko Shonin, established a temple called Jogyo-in in Kyoto, which later became known

Nine High Priests Come From Outside the Fuji School

as Yobo-ji. Originally a temple of the Fuji School, it gradually adopted practices such as worshiping Shakyamuni's statue and reciting the entire twenty-eight chapters of the Lotus Sutra. Eventually, Taiseki-ji refused to continue its relationship with Yobo-ji.

Nissho entered the priesthood at Yobo-ji when he was seven. There he received instruction from Nisshin, the nineteenth chief priest of Yobo-ji. After studying at a seminary in Shimosa province, he came to Taiseki-ji in August 1594. A mere two years later, in September 1596, he was appointed the fifteenth high priest.

For nearly one hundred years, from 1596 until 1692 when Nikkei transferred his office to Nichiei, the twenty-fourth high priest, Yobo-ji priests headed Taiseki-ji. In all, nine successive high priests from Nissho to Nikkei came from Yobo-ji. This demonstrates both Taiseki-ji's lack of capable priests

as well as its lenient attitude in maintaining doctrinal orthodoxy. The Yobo-ji priests brought unorthodox practices to
Taiseki-ji and distorted its teaching so much that Taiseki-ji
eventually allowed its branch temples to enshrine Shakyamuni's statue as an object of devotion.

Importation of its high priests from Yobo-ji invited long-
lasting criticism and ridicule. In October 1877, when some
members of a Yobo-ji branch temple converted to a Taiseki-ji
branch temple, they debated with a Yobo-ji priest through
correspondence. In one response, the Yobo-ji priest writes:

> Within the sect founded by Nikko Shonin, some
> temples, lacking in candidates for their chief priests,
> were compelled to ensure their succession by inviting
> priests from other branch schools. Naturally, as a re-
> sult, those temples brought the traditions from other
> branch schools into their own. Yobo-ji of Kyoto, how-
> ever, has not brought over priests of other branch
> schools in order to ensure its succession; it is the
> school of the true lineage from teacher to disciple, that
> is, Nichiren to Nikko, Nichimoku and Nichizon. . . .
>
> Since Taiseki-ji did not have candidates for its
> chief priest, upon its request, Yobo-ji dispatched the
> following nine to become its chief priest: Nissho, the
> fifteenth chief priest of Taiseki-ji; Nichiju, the six-
> teenth; Nissei, the seventeenth; Nichiei, the eigh-
> teenth; Nisshun, the nineteenth; Nitten, the twentieth;
> Nichinin, the twenty-first; Nisshun, the twenty-sec-
> ond; and Nikkei, the twenty-third.
>
> A pig may cost fifty yen, so nine would be 450 yen.
> But here we are talking about humans. At the request
> of Taiseki-ji, Yobo-ji sent full-fledged disciples trained

under High Priest Nisshin, who was a student of High Priest Nichizon, to Taiseki-ji as its successors so that they might be helpful. Oblivious to this, Taiseki-ji speaks ill of Yobo-ji; it is like an animal that does not know how to repay a debt of gratitude. (*EssentialWritings of the Fuji School*, vol. 7, p. 13)

In February 1602, when Nissho, the fifteenth high priest, was in office, Tokugawa Ieyasu established a shogunate government in Edo (present-day Tokyo). Around 1635, to solidify its control on the populace as well as to prevent the spread of Christianity, the Tokugawa government instituted a new Buddhist temple parish system. The system was established nationwide by 1638 when the Christian revolt in Shimabara was quelled. Under the parish system, people had to be registered with a Buddhist temple in their area to prove that they were not Christians. Unless they had a permit issued by their Buddhist temple, people were unable to work or travel. As people's lives essentially depended upon a temple permit, the authority of chief priests grew stronger. Even a parish leader, if he did not visit his temple on an appointed day, would have his name deleted from the register and reported to the government. Put simply, under the parish system, Buddhist temples functioned as a government census bureau to control people.

The Fuji School and Funeral Buddhism

The Tokugawa shogunate government also prohibited religious debate. No religious sect could publicly praise itself and criticize others. This government ordinance became effective around 1615. It prevented any overt religious propagation. Since the parish system made it extremely difficult for people to leave their parishes, their desire to improve their spiritual lives was greatly stifled, and Buddhism in Japan became increasingly conservative and ritualistic.

Since the government discouraged religious propagation, Buddhist temples started conducting more rituals to entice parish members to frequent their temples, thus generating income. Many temples, regardless of their sects, promoted rituals and formalities related to death—such as funerals; posthumous Buddhist names; memorial services; Buddhist tablets for the dead; thrice-yearly tomb visits in spring, summer and fall; and so on. For this reason, some critics, after the establishment of the parish system, refer to Japanese Buddhism as "funeral Buddhism."

The parish system also required that priests see their parish members when they died. Upon confirming that the deceased were in fact in his parish and not Christians, he would bestow upon them posthumous Buddhist names and recite prayers for their repose. Hence people were forced to invite priests to funerals. If they did not, they risked being labeled Christians and thus being executed.

It should also be noted that most of the Buddhist formalities surrounding funerals and memorial services were introduced during the seventeenth and eighteenth centuries. These required formalities included family tombs, memorial books, memorial tablets, Buddhist altars and so on. Parish members were required to make offerings to a priest at every service they attended. Furthermore, they were often asked to finance renovation and construction projects for their temples. People's discontent with the Buddhist clergy grew, and many sayings from the Edo period attest to the corruption of priests at that time: "All profit for priests." "If you hate a priest, you hate even his robe." "A priest recites a sutra only for what he is paid." "A priest snatches an offering without reciting a sutra." "Money talks even in hell." Even today it is customary to invite a priest to a funeral in Japan. This tradition, however, has nothing to do with any original Buddhist teaching or with one's enlightenment. It is a remnant of the parish system established by the Tokugawa shogunate government in the seventeenth century.

In June 1641, Nisshun, the nineteenth high priest, received from the newly appointed third shogun Tokugawa Iemitsu a deed reclaiming Taiseki-ji's property and its status as a head temple. At this time, Taiseki-ji also started to register its parish members and to vouch for their non-Christian status. Following the trend of the Buddhist community, Taiseki-ji stopped its propagation efforts and started to promote rituals and formalities such as funerals and memorial services. As a result, Taiseki-ji's parish members grew dependent on their priests and became negligent in their own personal practice, such as gongyo. Instead of doing gongyo, they would go to the temple and ask priests to pray on their behalf. This priest-based faith has since become the norm within the school headed by Taiseki-ji (eventually known as Nichiren Shoshu). Today Nichiren Shoshu priests still offer prayer services for lay believers: "prayer for health," "prayer for traffic safety," "prayer for warding off evils," "prayer for good grades" and so on.

Believers' dependency on priests is the antithesis of the self-reliant faith the Daishonin strongly advocates. He writes: "Muster your faith and pray to this Gohonzon. Then what is there that cannot be achieved?" (WND, 412). "The fact that her prayers have gone unanswered is like a strong bow with a weak bowstring, or a fine sword in the hands of a coward. It is in no sense the fault of the Lotus Sutra" (WND, 489). "No matter how earnestly Nichiren prays for you, if you lack faith, it will be like trying to set fire to wet tinder. Spur yourself to muster the power of faith (WND, 1000–01). And "Whether or not your prayer is answered will depend on your faith; [if it is not,] I will in no way be to blame" (WND, 1079). In light of these passages, it becomes evident that having a priest pray for one's happiness or enlightenment is contrary to the Daishonin's intent.

The government-instituted parish system encouraged further corruption in Japan's Buddhist community. Under strict government control and protection, the majority of Buddhist priests became oblivious to their role as spiritual teachers and increasingly became consumed with the pursuit of worldly fame and material gain. This is in exact accord with the Daishonin's premonition:

> The Buddha stated that, in the latter age, monks and nuns with the hearts of dogs would be as numerous as the sands of the Ganges. By this he meant that the priests and nuns of that day would be attached to fame and fortune. Because they wear robes and surplices, they look like ordinary priests and nuns. But in their hearts they wield a sword of distorted views, hastening here and there among their patrons and filling them with countless lies so as to keep them away from other priests or nuns. Thus they strive to keep their patrons to themselves and prevent other priests or nuns from coming near them, like a dog who goes to a house to be fed, but growls and springs to attack the moment another dog approaches. Each and every one of these priests and nuns is certain to fall into the evil paths. (WND, 755)

The parish system also helped the Buddhist clergy develop their sense of superiority over lay believers. Since priests essentially acted as government agents who held sway over people's lives, they viewed their relationship with their parish members as that between lord and serf. The Buddhist clergy's feudalistic view and people's acceptance of their spiritual serfdom persisted in Japan long after the priesthood's political influence disappeared with the demise of the Tokugawa shogunate government in the late nineteenth century.

CHAPTER 7

A High Priest Enshrines Shakymuni's Statue

The seventeenth high priest of Nichiren Shoshu, Nissei, is known for two major doctrinal errors. One was the establishment of a statue of Shakyamuni as an object of devotion, and the other was mandating that all twenty-eight chapters of the Lotus Sutra be recited in gongyo.

Nissei originally came from Yobo-ji temple, which had splintered from the Fuji School (see chapter 6 for further explanation). He became a disciple of Nichiju, the sixteenth high priest, who had also been a Yobo-ji priest. In 1632, Nichiju transferred his office to Nissei. The following year, Nissei transferred the office to Nichiei, the eighteenth high priest, who had been his senior at Yobo-ji.

But in 1637, due to Nichiei's illness (he died in 1638), Nissei returned to Taiseki-ji to assume the office of high priest once again. In the same year, Nissei received government permission to ride in a litter to the shogun's castle in Edo for an official audience with the shogun. This was a rare privilege, especially for a priest. The source of such privilege, as well as Nissei's increasing influence and rise to the office of high priest at Taiseki-ji, was the powerful patronage of Kyodai-in, the widow of Hachisuka Yoshishige, an influential governor of Awa province on Shikoku Island.

Nissei formed a close relationship with Kyodai-in, eight years his elder, considering her his "adopted mother." Kyodai-in built Hosho-ji in Edo to honor her husband, who died in 1620. In 1623, on the recommendation of Kyodai-in, Nissei became the chief priest of Hosho-ji. There he enshrined a statue of Shakyamuni as an object of devotion and encouraged the recitation of the entire Lotus Sutra. In 1633, one year after he became high priest, he wrote a thesis later known as "Zuigi Ron," attempting to justify his unorthodox practices and silence the criticism brought against him. He writes at the end of the "Zuigi Ron": "A year after the completion of Hosho-ji, I had a statue of the Buddha made. Priests and lay believers of this school then brought up questions and criticism. To dispel the mist of their delusion and to avoid sinking into oblivion, I took up the writing brush to put down this one volume" (*Essential Writings of the Fuji School*, vol. 9, p. 69).

In his thesis, Nissei explains that Nichiren Daishonin did not establish Shakyamuni's statue as an object of devotion simply because he constantly had to move from one place to another; it was never his intent not to establish Shakyamuni's statue. Later Nichiin, the thirty-first high priest, added his commentary at the end of the thesis, stating that Nissei's doctrines "differ greatly from the essential teachings of this school."

Regarding Nissei's errors, Nichiko Hori, the fifty-ninth high priest, states: "As Nissei established the foundation in Edo and started to build branch temples there to increase the sect's influence, he at last began propounding the worship of the Buddha's statue and the recitation of the entire Lotus Sutra, thus bringing into [this school] the doctrine that Yobo-ji was then propounding" (*Essential Writings of the Fuji*

School, vol. 9, p. 69). Shakyamuni's statues were enshrined at many branch temples—including Hosho-ji, Josen-ji, Seiryu-ji, Myokyo-ji, Honjo-ji, Kujo-ji, Choan-ji, Kujo-ji and Hongen-ji (*Essential Writings of the Fuji School,* vol. 9, pp. 69–70). Among these only Josen-ji and Myokyo-ji exist today. Another record shows that Shakyamuni's statues were enshrined at one point at Jozai-ji and Jitsujo-ji. Nissei erected Shakyamuni's statue at more than ten branch temples over which he had influence.

Nikko Shonin left Mount Minobu because of the doctrinal errors committed by Hakiri Sanenaga, the steward of the Minobu area, including Hakiri's establishing Shakyamuni's statue as an object of devotion. Nikko Shonin maintained that only the Gohonzon should be the object of devotion. Nikko Shonin foresaw the appearance of aberrant high priests such as Nissei in the future and wrote: "Do not follow even the high priest if he goes against the Buddha's Law and propounds his own views" (GZ, 1618).

Some priests and lay believers raised concerns over the high priest's new practices, but no one followed Nikko Shonin's injunction by refusing to follow Nissei. In fact, since Taiseki-ji was increasing its branch temples and adding many buildings on the head temple grounds through the efforts of Kyodai-in, Nissei was later regarded as a "restorer" of the Fuji School.

As quickly as Nissei had risen to the office of high priest and enjoyed rare privileges in the shogun's court through the patronage of Kyodai-in, his status fell when he argued with his powerful patron. In 1638, Nissei and Kyodai-in had a

Powerful Lay Patron Appoints High Priest

falling out, so he left Taiseki-ji suddenly and moved to Jozai-ji at Shitaya in Edo. Taiseki-ji was without a high priest for three years from 1638 to 1641 until Nisshun, the nineteenth high priest, arrived to assume the office. The biographical account of Nisshun states:

> Because of his discord with the Venerable Priestess Nissho [Kyodai-in], a great patron, Teacher Nissei of the head temple left Mount Fuji and moved to Jozai-ji at Shitaya in Edo, thus leaving the head temple without its chief priest.
>
> At that time, with the appointment of a new shogun, the government had to reissue the deed [for the head temple's property], yet there was no chief priest, so the head temple was about to be condemned.
>
> Distressed by this, priests and lay believers entreated Venerable Priestess Nissho for her help regarding the appointment of the next chief priest. The venerable priestess was to choose one.
>
> Nikkan, then chief priest of Hosho-ji temple, told her that there was no one like Nisshun. Thus the venerable priestess invited Teacher [Nisshun] to the head temple. (*Essential Writings of the Fuji School*, vol. 5, p. 269)

So Nisshun went to Taiseki-ji to assume the office of high priest in 1641. Put simply, the powerful lay patron Kyodai-in in effect appointed the high priest. The head temple could then renew the deed to its property and maintain its status as a head temple. If Taiseki-ji had remained without a high priest, the Fuji School would have lost its independent status and become a branch temple of some other sect.

The transfer of the office of high priest from Nissei to

Nisshun, however, did not take place until October 27, 1645. The biographical account of Nisshun states:

> Later a reconciliation between Teacher Nissei and the venerable priestess [Kyodai-in] was realized, and the trust and respect between them were restored as it was before. So in the second year of Shoho [1645], Teacher Nissei went to the head temple and, on the twenty-seventh day of the tenth month of the same year, [Teacher Nisshun] received from Teacher Nissei the great transmission of the Golden Utterance of the Buddha and thus officially became the nineteenth high priest. (*Essential Writings of the Fuji School*, vol. 5, p. 270)

As mentioned here, Nisshun was a "high priest without the lineage" for about four years. It is also recorded that Nisshun transcribed Gohonzon in January and February of 1645. So it is noteworthy that without the formal transfer of the lineage of high priest, one could assume the office and conduct its various administrative responsibilities, including transcription of the Gohonzon. This is yet another historical fact that contradicts the current Nichiren Shoshu priesthood's assertion that only a legitimate high priest can transcribe Gohonzon and confer them upon believers, thanks to the mystical spiritual property called the "Living Essence" that he received from his predecessor through the transfer ceremony (*The Liturgy of Nichiren Shoshu*, Nichiren Shoshu Head Temple Taiseki-ji edition, English version, p. 35).

Because of the unusual circumstances surrounding Nisshun's appointment, some criticism and opposition were expected. So when Nisshun was invited to Taiseki-ji, Nikkan, then chief priest of Hosho-ji in Edo, who had recommended Nisshun to Kyodai-in, sent the following letter to the high priest:

> At Taiseki-ji, the heritage of the Law is transmitted through the Golden Utterance of the Buddha. One who receives this transmission—whether he is learned or un-learned—is a living person of Shakyamuni and Nichiren. Only by putting faith in this can people of the Latter Day sow the seed of Buddhahood. . . . Whoever becomes high priest, as long as he received the transmission of the heritage of the Law, should be known as a living person of Shakyamuni and Nichiren. This is the true intent of the founder [of Taiseki-ji, Nikko Shonin] and the basis for the school's believers. (*Essential Writings of the Fuji School*, vol. 5, p. 271)

To solidify support for Nisshun, the absolute authority of high priest was once again invoked by equating the successive high priests with the Daishonin. The recorded history of the Fuji School demonstrates that the high priest's infallibility was advocated not because the high priest was worthy of respect; rather, this unorthodox doctrine was used as convenient dogma to silence criticism against the high priest and bolster his influence.

Even after he relinquished his office, Nissei continued to enjoy some influence in the Fuji School. Many branch temples continued to enshrine Shakyamuni's statue. Only after Nissei's death in 1683 could Nisshun, the twenty-second high priest [a different person from the nineteenth high priest, whose name is pronounced the same yet spelled with different Chinese characters], and Nikkei, the twenty-third high priest, both of whom originally came from Yobo-ji, remove Shakyamuni's statues from Taiseki-ji's branch temples.

Shakyamuni's statues were enshrined as objects of devotion for nearly fifty years at some branch temples and even sixty years at others. Even after the removal of those statues, Yobo-ji's influence continued to be felt in the Fuji School until Nichikan, the twenty-sixth high priest, thoroughly refuted its teachings.

CHAPTER 8

Nichikan: Restorer of the Fuji School

The twenty-sixth high priest, Nichikan (1665–1726), is known as the great restorer of the Fuji School because he refuted erroneous beliefs and traditions brought into the school by his predecessors from Yobo-ji (see chapters 6 and 7 for more information). These teachings and practices were contrary to those established by Nichiren Daishonin, and Nichikan saw that correction was urgently needed.

Refutation of Erroneous Teachings

Born into a family of the samurai class, Nichikan entered the priesthood at eighteen and studied under Nichiei, the twenty-fourth high priest. At twenty-four, he went to the Hosokusa Seminary to study further. The Hosokusa Seminary was established jointly by Taiseki-ji and the Eight Chapters School, which maintained that the Daishonin's core teaching lay in eight chapters of the Lotus Sutra—the fifteenth through the twenty-second. After nine years, Nichikan became a professor at the seminary.

He later moved to Taiseki-ji and lived in Renzo-bo, a lodging temple on the head temple grounds. He assumed the important position of study master, generally held by those considered candidates for the office of high priest. In 1718, he became the twenty-sixth high priest.

Nichikan practiced and studied diligently in his efforts to clarify the Daishonin's Buddhism. He lectured and wrote extensively on the Daishonin's writings and completed his most vital work, *The Six-volume Writings*, in 1725. The purpose of this work was to refute the erroneous doctrines of the various Nichiren schools and clarify the orthodoxy of the Daishonin's Buddhism. These six volumes include: "The Threefold Secret Teachings," "Meanings Hidden in the Depths," "Interpretations Based on the Law," "Teaching for the Latter Day," "The Practice of This School" and "The Three Robes of This School."

In "Teaching for the Latter Day," Nichikan specifically took up the doctrines propounded by Nisshin (1508–76) of Yobo-ji. In the first half, he points out the errors of reciting the entire twenty-eight chapters of the Lotus Sutra. In the latter half, he refutes the practice of worshipping statues of Shakyamuni Buddha. By correcting Nisshin's teachings, Nichikan purged Taiseki-ji of the unorthodoxy espoused by previous high priests who had been influenced by Yobo-ji. By the time Nichikan became high priest, some four hundred years after the Daishonin's passing, Nichiren schools had distorted his teachings and promulgated various misinterpretations. Through the *Six-volume Writings*, Nichikan reestablished the orthodoxy of the Daishonin's Buddhism as transmitted to his legitimate successor, Nikko Shonin.

According to "The Accounts of High Priest Nichikan," when Nichikan bestowed the *Six-volume Writings* on his disciples, he stated: "With these six volumes of writing, which are like the lion king, you need not be afraid of the various sects and schools in the nation even if they all come to this temple for debate like a pack of foxes. . ." (*Essential Writings of the Fuji School*, vol. 5, pp. 355–56).

Nichikan believed that the purpose of Buddhist study was to propagate the Daishonin's Buddhism. In the beginning of "The Threefold Secret Teaching," he states: "There are many important matters in this writing. This I did solely to perpetuate the Law. My disciples should deeply understand my intention" (*Six-volume Writings*, p. 3).

He begins "Interpretations Based on the Law" by stating: "This is solely for the sake of the widespread propagation of the Law" (ibid., p. 115).

Through his writings, Nichikan reconfirmed the basics of faith, practice and study. He clarified Nichiren Daishonin as the original Buddha of the Latter Day of the Law and the Gohonzon as the basis of faith. Through his efforts came a period of unprecedented development in Buddhist study. Many student priests traveled to the Fuji School to further their studies.

Nichikan also contributed greatly to the construction of buildings on the grounds of Taiseki-ji. He oversaw the construction of a main gate and reception hall on the temple grounds. He built the Ever-Chanting Hall and a lodging temple, the Ishino-bo. He also left behind the funds later used for the construction of the Five-Storied Pagoda, which was completed in 1749 during the tenure of the thirty-first high priest, Nichiin.

According to "The Accounts of High Priest Nichikan," on August 19, 1726, Nichikan died peacefully after enjoying his favorite meal of buckwheat noodles. After dinner, he declared cheerfully, "How wonderful the City of Tranquil Light is!" then chanted daimoku (*Essential Writings of the Fuji School*, vol. 5, p. 359).

Nichiko Hori, the fifty-ninth high priest, said of Nichikan:

It was said that Teacher Nichikan was held in such high esteem that the day would not break nor the night fall without his presence. This was due to his behavior and character rather than his scholarship, for one cannot command trust from the priesthood and laity if he is lax in everyday conduct regardless of his achievements in Buddhist study and debate. In this regard, Teacher Nichikan was extremely modest and honest. I believe this is why Teacher Nichikan's faith, let alone his understanding of Buddhism, flowed through the people. (*The Daibyakurenge*, November 1956, p. 20)

Nichikan gained the respect and trust of those who knew him, and that is how he reestablished the Daishonin's correct spirit in the hearts of believers. Nichikan's life was eloquent proof that a high priest of outstanding faith, practice and study as well as outstanding character need not invoke the mysterious "transmission of the Law" to support his office or promote his alleged infallibility.

Nichikan viewed study as a means to deepen faith and practice—never for merely displaying one's knowledge. At the end of his commentary on the Daishonin's "On Practicing the Buddha's Teachings," he states:

Emphasis on the Basics of Faith and Practice

If we do not constantly ponder the four dictums[1] and if we ignore propagation, our hearts will become accomplices in slandering the Law. If we do not accomplish propagation with our voices, they will become accomplices in the slander of the Law. If we do not face the object of devotion with prayer beads in our hands, our bodies will become accomplices in the slander of the Law. Therefore, those who ponder the object of devotion of the essential teaching of the Lotus Sutra face the object of devotion of the "Life Span" chapter of the essential teaching and chant Nam-myoho-renge-kyo of the actual three thousand realms in a single moment of life —that is, the Buddhism of sowing contained in the "Life Span" chapter of the essential teaching of the Lotus Sutra—shall be the ones propagating the Law through the three types of karma—thoughts, words and deeds. (*The Collection of High Priest Nichikan's Commentaries*, p. 767)

Nichikan teaches us that our basic practice lies in gongyo, daimoku and teaching others the greatness of Nichiren Daishonin's Buddhism. He warns that when we become slack in this basic practice, we develop a tendency to go against the Law.

Nichikan also expounds on the meaning of chanting daimoku:

So know that the daimoku of true Buddhism must be accompanied by faith and practice. The chanting of Nam-myoho-renge-kyo with faith in the object of devotion of true Buddhism shall be known as the daimoku of true Buddhism. But although there is faith, if it lacks practice, it shall not yet be known as such. . . . Therefore, be aware that the daimoku of true Buddhism shall be the kind that encompasses both faith and practice. (*Six-volume Writings*, p. 107)

The twenty-sixth high priest explains that chanting Nam-myoho-renge-kyo cannot be called a correct practice of the Daishonin's teaching unless it is accompanied by sincere faith in the Gohonzon and concrete actions for the propagation of Buddhism.

Commenting on the passage *simply chanting the daimoku* from the Daishonin's "The Daimoku of the Lotus Sutra" (WND, 141), Nichikan states: "Here 'simply chanting the daimoku' means to chant with faith. If one chants the Mystic Law without faith, it is not called chanting the daimoku" (*The Collection of High Priest Nichikan's Commentaries*, p. 639). He reiterates the point that no matter how much we chant Nam-myoho-renge-kyo to the Gohonzon, if we lack faith, all our efforts will be to no avail.

In October 1993, the SGI began conferring Gohonzon transcribed by Nichikan upon its worldwide membership. This

SGI's Conferral of the Nichikan Gohonzon

was in response to the excommunication of the SGI by Nikken Abe, the sixty-seventh high priest, who then ceased issuing Gohonzon to SGI members unless they left the SGI and joined the temple. Sendo Narita, chief priest of Joen-ji in Tochigi, Japan, who had renounced his affiliation with Taiseki-ji in protest, proposed to the SGI that a Nichikan-transcribed Gohonzon at his temple be reproduced and made available. The SGI accepted this proposal.

The Daishonin writes: "Nichiren has been trying to awaken all the people of Japan to faith in the Lotus Sutra so that they too can share the heritage and attain Buddhahood" (WND, 217). He inscribed the Gohonzon for this purpose—that all people can receive the heritage of the Law and attain Buddhahood.

In this regard, Nichikan comments:

All those who accept and embrace this object of devotion will enter the Buddha Way of time without beginning. . . . The bodies of us ordinary people who enter the Buddha Way of time without beginning are exactly the Buddhas of absolute freedom from time without beginning. The entity of the Buddha of absolute freedom is nothing other than us ordinary people. . . . This is what is meant by the oneness of mentor and disciple. (*The Collection of High Priest Nichikan's Commentaries*, p. 488)

Through our faith and practice to the Gohonzon, our lives reveal the life of the Buddha of absolute freedom; that is, a state of life no different from that of Nichiren Daishonin. This, Nichikan stresses, is the meaning of the oneness of mentor and disciple. The heritage of the Daishonin's Buddhism, therefore, is nothing other than faith in the Gohonzon. It is the lifeblood of faith that enables us to attain Buddhahood.

The mission of the Daishonin's disciples lies in spreading his teaching so that many people may take faith in the Gohonzon and attain Buddhahood, thus creating the basis for a peaceful society. The fact that Nikken excommunicated the SGI, which has been propagating the Daishonin's teaching on a global scale, clearly demonstrates that he has renounced the mission of the Daishonin's disciple as well as the role of high priest. In this context and to fulfill its mission, the SGI began conferring the Nichikan-transcribed Gohonzon for the further spread of the Daishonin's Buddhism.

The Nichiren Shoshu priesthood criticizes the SGI's

conferral of the Gohonzon, claiming that unless conferred by the high priest, Gohonzon are devoid of the heritage of the Law and have no beneficial power. But the tradition to entrust the high priest at Taiseki-ji with the transcription and conferral of Gohonzon was to protect the integrity of the Daishonin's Buddhism and further promote its widespread propagation. It was never meant to create a privileged class of clergy with the power to manipulate believers with the Gohonzon. Neither was the tradition meant to allow the clergy to exploit believers financially through the conferral of the Gohonzon.

Nichiren Daishonin writes, "Even embracing the Lotus Sutra would be useless without the heritage of faith" (WND, 218). Those who lack faith and make no effort to spread the Law, not to mention deliberately obstructing its propagation, cannot receive the heritage of this Buddhism. This is why the current priesthood has lost its qualification to reproduce and confer Gohonzon.

The heritage of the Daishonin's Buddhism exists only in the selfless dedication to kosen-rufu of millions of SGI members. That the Nichikan-transcribed Gohonzon issued by the SGI are in accord with the Daishonin's teaching and spirit is also proven by the benefits the members have received.

The priesthood's assertion that the SGI-issued Gohonzon are counterfeit because they are not sanctioned and consecrated by the high priest or issued by the head temple contradicts its own recorded history. Up until the mid-1950s, a number of branch temples reproduced Gohonzon transcribed by past high priests with whom they had strong ties. These branch temples then freely issued those Gohonzon to their parish members. Of course those branch temples never asked for the high priest's permission, nor did the high priest perform the so-called eye-opening ceremony upon those Gohonzon to consecrate them.

Even after the head temple established its sole authority to reproduce and confer Gohonzon in the 1960s, the high priest did not perform an eye-opening ceremony on every Gohonzon issued. In fact, priests have testified that most Gohonzon were shipped out of the head temple without receiving the high priest's consecration. Now they claim it is essential to infuse the Gohonzon with the power derived from the "Living Essence" of the Daishonin, which is possessed only by the high priest. There is no record in any of the Daishonin's writings that he performed an eye-opening ceremony on the Gohonzon. Nor did he mention anywhere that it is necessary.

The Gohonzon is already the embodiment of the Mystic Law; it is already the eye of all Buddhas with which to perceive our own Buddha nature. What draws upon the power of the Buddha and the power of the Law in the Gohonzon is our own powers of faith and practice. When those dedicated to the spread of Buddhism pray to the Gohonzon with sincere faith, they manifest the same state of life as Nichiren Daishonin.

---

1. Four dictums: Also called the four maxims. Four statements with which Nichiren Daishonin denounced the four most influential Buddhist sects of his day, summarizing his repudiation of their doctrines. They are: 1.) "Nembutsu leads to the hell of incessant suffering," 2.) "Zen is the teaching of devils," 3.) "Shingon will ruin the nation," and 4.) "Ritsu is traitorous."

CHAPTER 9

Persecutions in the Eighteenth and Nineteenth Centuries

In the early eighteenth century, many samurai under Maeda Tsunanori, governor of the Kaga, Noto and Etchu provinces,

The Kanazawa Persecution

converted to Nichiren Daishonin's Buddhism. They did so after attending sermons at Jozai-ji, a branch temple of the Fuji School in present-day Tokyo.

Upon their return to Kanazawa, the capital of Kaga, they propagated their new faith among retainers of the Maeda clan. This is believed to be the beginning of the spread of the Daishonin's teachings in Kanazawa. But because of the restrictions of the parish system, they could not openly convert to the Fuji School and had to conceal their faith from government officials and priests of other temples. Under the government-instituted parish system (see chapter 7 for more information) in Japan, citizens were legally bound for life to the temple of their parents and ancestors.

In 1726, Ryomyo, a priest of Jiun-ji, a Nichiren School temple, converted to the Fuji School while traveling to further his studies of the Daishonin's Buddhism. He then entered the school's Hosokusa Seminary. Ryomyo's conversion, however, became an issue in local religious circles. There was no branch temple of the Fuji School in the Kaga areas governed by the Maeda family, so converts had no temple with which to register.

Furthermore, priests from the Minobu branch of the Nichiren School reported to the provincial authorities that the Fuji School was very similar to the Fuju-fuse branch, which had already been outlawed by the government. The Fuju-fuse School had a policy of not making or accepting contributions to or from those it regarded as heretics, which was highly offensive to the authorities. As a result, the Maeda clan issued an edict that outlawed the Fuji School as well, concerned that its apparent similarity to the outlawed Fuju-fuse School would cause confusion within local parishes (*Essential Writings of the Fuji School*, vol. 9, p. 278).

The Daishonin explains the inevitable persecution that those who propagate his Buddhism will face, stating: "If you propagate it, devils will arise without fail. If they did not, there would be no way of knowing that this is the correct teaching" (WND, 501). For the believers in Kanazawa, it came in the form of suppression by their local government.

In 1727, twenty-eighth high priest Nissho sent a request to the governor asking for a permit to build a temple in the area to support the growing number of believers. But Nissho's request was denied. In the petition, Nissho mentions that "those who took faith for the last few decades number several thousand" (*Essential Writings of the Fuji School*, vol. 9, p. 293). In spite of the persecution befalling them, there were a substantial number of believers in the Kanazawa area.

Nissho could have appealed the governor's decision to the shogunate government, but decided against it. Nichiko Hori, the fifty-ninth high priest, speculated as to why Nissho did not file an appeal and persist in the efforts to construct a temple in the area. Nissho, he points out, probably was "concerned about bringing danger to his own temple" as well as "the possibility of believers in Kanazawa being subjected to more severe punishment" (ibid., vol. 9, p. 291).

While the head temple failed to extend any further support, believers in Kanazawa continued to practice and spread the Daishonin's Buddhism. Despite the ban issued by the authorities, believers did organize themselves. Historical records indicate that there were at least thirteen lay organizations of the Fuji School in the area. Those believers propagated the Daishonin's teaching and encouraged one another without any support from the priesthood. They also exerted themselves in Buddhist study. About four hundred books on Buddhism copied by the believers in Kanazawa still exist. In June 1749, when Taiseki-ji built its Five-Storied Pagoda, Kanazawa members donated a large sum of money —more than three hundred *ryo* (a monetary unit in thirteenth-century Japan)—to the priesthood, despite having been left to fend for themselves.

Toward the end of 1770, the ruling Maeda family again issued a ban on the religious practice of Taiseki-ji and the Fuji School. At that time, seven or eight leading believers, including Nishida Joemon and Takeuchi Hachiemon, were sentenced to various punishments. Most of them were low-ranking samurai serving the Maeda family and were eventually pardoned three years later.

But Joemon, who had exerted himself in propagation for thirty years and had helped form two lay organizations, died of an illness while serving his sentence. In March 1786, Hachiemon was again summoned by the provincial officials, who demanded that he renounce his faith. When he refused to do so, he was imprisoned and died in prison on April 29 of the same year. Records show that several hundred fellow practitioners attended his funeral to honor a life dedicated to the spread of the Daishonin's Buddhism.

There were about twelve thousand people in Kanazawa and surrounding areas practicing the Daishonin's Buddhism. The office of religious affairs, which enforced the parish system, was clearly alarmed by the rapid growth of the Fuji School. In July 1786, seven leading believers, including Nakamura Kohei, were arrested and questioned by the provincial government. Nakamura Kohei, representing the believers, responded to government officials during the examination. He was pressured to reveal the names of those who practiced with the Fuji School but refused, stating: "Out of respect for the government system, I wish to remain silent [about the outlawed faith]. Since I do not know who practices the faith, it would be difficult to tell" (ibid., vol. 9, p. 305). He did explain how he had taken faith in the Daishonin's teachings and how he believed his faith helped him serve his lord.

Nakamura Kohei was summoned several more times after that, but he refused to give up his faith. He went so far as to submit a letter of remonstration proclaiming that "the faith of the Taiseki-ji School is in accord with the time and conditions of the Latter Day of the Law" and that "if the true object of devotion is abandoned and thus the True Law becomes extinct, the [Maeda] family would not prosper" (*The Records of the Kanazawa Persecution*, p. 87). On September 26, 1786, Nakamura Kohei was imprisoned. Later, on December 23, he was pardoned and returned to work. This was the last recorded incident of the Kanazawa Persecution.

The propagation efforts of ordinary people brought about the Kanazawa Persecution. In its course, five believers were imprisoned, with one of them dying in confinement; fourteen were placed under house arrest; and many were harshly interrogated. The priesthood at Taiseki-ji, on the other hand, submitted one petition to build a branch temple in the Kanazawa area and thereafter remained silent. Eventually the enthusiasm of Kanazawa believers died down, and by the time Taiseki-ji finally established a temple nearly one hundred years later in November 1879, only eighty households remained. Only 150 people attended the opening.

In May 1784, believers in Ina, Shinano province, came under government persecution. Jokura Mozaemon was a farmer in

The Ina Persecution

Koide Village in Ina. Although his family had for generations belonged to Jorin-ji, a Zen temple, he eventually chose to practice at Jinmyo-ji, a Nichiren School temple. In 1763, when he was nineteen, he determined to visit one thousand temples related to Nichiren Buddhism. During this trip, Mozaemon encountered the correct teaching of the Daishonin at Taiseki-ji and converted to the Fuji School. Upon his return to Ina, he began to spread the Daishonin's teaching based on this school. It was a time of many natural disasters, and people were receptive to the Daishonin's teachings.

As more people began to practice, Mozaemon built a small hall on his estate for his fellow believers to gather and chant daimoku. Alarmed by the increasing number of Fuji School believers, three temples—Kokyu-ji and Jorin-ji of the Soto branch of the Zen School and Jinmyo-ji of another Nichiren school—lodged a complaint with the local government. In response, the office of religious affairs of the provincial government sent out some thirty men to arrest three leading believers—Mozaemon, Saheiji and Tozaemon.

They were imprisoned on the suspicion of being Christians. Apparently the priests had complained to the provincial government that they were Christians—the practice of Christianity being illegal. For three days the authorities attempted to torture a confession out of Mozaemon. He was forced to kneel on sharp wooden planks, his head was submerged in water nearly to the point of drowning, and he was forced to drink an excessive amount of water. It is recorded that "No matter how severely he was tortured, he continued to chant daimoku as long as he could breathe" (*Essential Writings of the Fuji School*, vol. 9, p. 410). Since the government could not find any evidence that he practiced Christianity, Mozaemon escaped the death sentence. But he and his family had their house and fields confiscated and were exiled from the village. Some other believers were placed under house arrest. The priests of the three temples were also placed under house arrest for lodging a false complaint.

Twenty-three years later, Mozaemon was pardoned and returned to Ina. For the next one hundred-some years, the believers of Ina continued to gather to chant daimoku and study the Daishonin's writings. Unlike the Kanazawa Persecution of believers in the samurai class, the Ina Persecution was prompted by the propagation efforts of farmers and peasants. Meanwhile, the priesthood at Taiseki-ji remained silent throughout the affair.

It was ordinary people who first propagated the Daishonin's teachings in Owari province (present-day Aichi Prefecture)

The Owari Persecution   as well—particularly in the area around Nagoya. Around 1822, toward the end of the rule of the Tokugawa shogunate, a lay believer named Nagase Seijuro, from Meguro in Edo (present-day Tokyo), went to Owari province to spread the Daishonin's teaching even though there was no Fuji School temple there.

When he was young, Seijuro was a believer of the Minobu branch of the Nichiren School. Later he converted to Taiseki-ji. He often traveled from northeastern Honshu (Japan's main island) to the Owari area in central Honshu to spread the Daishonin's teaching. He also excelled in religious debate. Around 1830, he won a debate with an influential believer of the Minobu branch. (This debate is known as the Sunamura Debate.)

Takasaki Tayo, a woman who had been converted by Seijuro, led propagation efforts in the Owari area. She established a women's lay organization. Her son Takasaki Katsuji, who was a retainer of the ruling Tokugawa family of Owari province, also exerted himself in propagation and established a lay organization. With these efforts, the number of believers in the Owari area increased dramatically.

Seijuro also went to the Hokuzai area of Nagoya (present-day Komaki, Inuyama and Kasugai cities) to spread the Daishonin's teaching. In this area, Funabashi Gizaemon, Hiramatsu Masuemon, Kimata Ukyo and Iwata Rizo led the propagation campaign. They were all ordinary citizens — farmers and merchants — but they were well educated. Since they had been believers of a Nichiren School, they had some foundation in Buddhist study. Once they were awakened to the orthodox teachings of the Fuji School, they became a driving force behind propagation in their area.

They also challenged priests and lay believers of the various Nichiren schools, such as the Minobu branch, the Kenpon Hokke branch and the Eight Chapters branch, in religious debate and repeatedly defeated them. This caused those various Nichiren schools to lodge complaints with the provincial government's office of religious affairs. Such complaints prompted the local government to persecute the believers in Owari four times over a fifty-year period.

In 1825 and 1826, local officials raided believers' homes in the Hokuzai area of Nagoya and confiscated the Gohonzon. In those raids, believers were beaten and kicked. Funabashi Gizaemon was the main target of the raids.

In the fall of 1837, after an initial series of raids, believers became cautious and hid their Gohonzon behind statues of the Buddha in their altars. But Hiramatsu Masuemon had his Buddhist altar examined by local officials and was immediately arrested. He was taken to the office of religious affairs and interrogated for an extended period. Iwata Rizo and Kimata Ukyo experienced similar treatment. These incidents took place repeatedly until the spring of the following year.

For eight years, from 1847 to 1854, persecutions intensified. Each year Fuji School believers suffered some form of harassment from the provincial government. In February 1848, Kimata Ukyo completely refuted Chijo-in, a Myoraku-ji priest, in a religious debate. Incensed, Chijo-in demanded that Kimata Ukyo and his son Sakyo submit a letter of apology. The priest also attempted to have Ukyo's job at a local Shinto shrine taken away.

On August 25 of the same year, Kimata Ukyo was summoned to Hon'en-ji by someone claiming to act on the authority of the office of religious affairs and was detained there. On August 29, Kimata, along with Iwata Rizo and Zen'noemon, was transported to the office of religious affairs, escorted by eighty-some Minobu priests and lay believers. There they were flogged, beaten and tortured by local officials.

On September 9, Zen'noemon was released and returned

to his village, sick and beaten almost to death. The government regarded Ukyo and Rizo as ringleaders and detained them for further interrogation. Meanwhile, Hiramatsu Masuemon petitioned a steward of the ruling family. The steward was moved by the plight of these believers and issued a warning to the office of religious affairs. As a result, on September 27, Ukyo was released, and on October 4, Rizo returned to his village. Both had to be carried home in a litter. On October 22 and 23, Masuemon was summoned and questioned by local officials.

Masuemon, Rizo and Ukyo then had a religious debate with high-ranking priests of the officially sanctioned temples of the various Nichiren schools. These schools worked closely with the office of religious affairs. The debate was held in three sessions—October 25, November 2 and November 10 —under the supervision of the office of religious affairs.

Through this debate the provincial government sought to convert the leading believers of the Fuji School to other Nichiren schools in the area. However, the lay believers led by Rizo refuted the priests' arguments and pointed out their errors one by one. In many instances, the priests were unable to respond. Furthermore, to the embarrassment of the debating priests, some priests in the audience acknowledged the points argued by Rizo and others.

Their arguments compelled the priests to accept the two transfer documents that validate Nikko Shonin as the legitimate successor of the Daishonin and confirmed the slanderous nature of actions by Hakiri Sanenaga, the steward of Minobu, which prompted Nikko Shonin to leave the area. Through the debate, known as the Owari Debate, the lay believers of the Fuji School affirmed the orthodoxy of the Daishonin's Buddhism.

Regarding the Owari Debate, Nichiko Hori writes: "The debate ended in triumph for the lay believers of the Fuji School and in miserable defeat for the officially sanctioned temples. The fact that the positions of priests as teachers and lay believers as students were completely reversed brought public honor to the three [lay believers] and indelible disgrace to the seven temples. Furthermore, [at the debate] government officials heard that the faith of the Fuji School is not erroneous but is the orthodox and correct teaching among all Nichiren schools" (*History of the Owari Persecution*, p. 85).

After the Owari Debate, Rizo and Kimata Sakyo, the son of Ukyo, led propagation efforts. In 1854, Sakyo refuted the priests of Gyokuzen-ji concerning the relative merits of the theoretical teaching (or first half) of the Lotus Sutra and its essential teaching (or latter half). After Sakyo's victory, more people took faith in the Fuji School throughout the Owari area.

As propagation progressed, another persecution occurred in 1858 in the Komeno area of Owari province. On November 8, about thirty villagers were arrested. Three of them were severely tortured. The local government continued to harass Fuji School believers in Owari province until 1876, when the new Meiji government issued an edict ensuring religious freedom.

During the eighteenth and nineteenth centuries, ordinary people of Kanazawa, Ina and Owari awakened to the Daishonin's Buddhism and enthusiastically spread their faith. Threatened by the rapid increase in the number of believers, influential priests of other schools instigated persecution by local officials. Despite this, many believers courageously continued their faith.

On the other hand, the priesthood at Taiseki-ji, fearful of

persecution and concerned about self-preservation, remained silent and kept its distance from the laity. While approximately a hundred believers were subjected to persecution for their efforts to spread the Daishonin's Buddhism during the Edo period (1603–1867), only two priests in the remote Sendai area were persecuted for propagation. In view of the above events under the parish system instituted in this period, it is evident that the priesthood at Taiseki-ji had grown more concerned about its own survival than the spread of the Daishonin's teaching.

CHAPTER 10

The Priesthood Renounces Celibacy

In December 1866, imperial rule was restored in Japan. The following January, the imperial army defeated the army of the Tokugawa shogunate at Toba and Fushimi near Kyoto. In September, the era name was changed to Meiji after the reigning emperor, and the imperial palace moved from Kyoto (whose name means "capital city") to Edo, which was then renamed Tokyo ("eastern capital"). During this tumultuous time of civil war leading to the inauguration of the imperial Meiji government, the Fuji School at Taiseki-ji was headed by Nichiden, its fifty-second high priest.

Starting in the Nineteenth Century, Priests Are Allowed To Marry

On April 25, 1872, the Meiji government issued a decree that would drastically transform the Buddhist clergy of Japan. It states in part: "Priests may eat meat, get married and grow their hair." The decree also allowed priests to wear regular clothing instead of Buddhist robes and surplices when they were not attending religious services. From this time on, the majority of priests in Japan openly renounced the time-honored monastic tradition of celibacy and began to marry.

Concerned about the demoralizing effect this might have on the Buddhist community, some priests strongly protested the decree and demanded that the government retract it. In February 1878, the government issued a notice clarifying that its decree was intended to lift the bans (on meat-eating, marriage and hair growth by priests) instituted by the shogunate government but not to force Buddhist schools to change their monastic rules. In other words, the government maintained that it was up to the priests themselves to decide if they were to eat meat, have wives and grow hair. But this notice came too late to reverse the trend. Most Buddhist priests at that time gladly took the government decree as an excuse to renounce celibacy. They saw the rules on sexual conduct as oppressive government restrictions on their private lives rather than as self-imposed rules derived from the Buddhist monastic tradition.

During the Edo period, the shogunate government monitored the activities of priests in order to maintain strict control of the Buddhist clergy and thereby ensure the effectiveness of the parish system. When priests were found to have had a sexual relationship with a woman, they were severely punished. If the guilty priest was the chief priest of a temple, he was exiled to a remote island. In the case of student priests, they were placed in stocks for public viewing and later expelled from their temples.

Once the restrictions were lifted by the new regime, priests gladly started to marry. This is a clear indication that the Buddhist community had lost the integrity to decide on matters of Buddhist tradition. Instead, priests regarded the government as the legitimate authority over their traditions.

Put simply, the years of strict government control had made the Buddhist clergy entirely dependent on political authority. Some contend that the Meiji government issued the decree to enfeeble the morale of the Buddhist community and thereby elevate Shinto, which was viewed as the chief means of extolling imperial authority.

Nichiden criticized priests of other Buddhist schools for their elation over the government decree, regarding it as an expression of imperial mercy. He stated that despite the trend in the Buddhist community, the priesthood of the Fuji School should uphold the precepts of the Daishonin and Nikko Shonin and remain celibate. But eventually the priesthood at Taiseki-ji succumbed to the trend.

The priesthood's renouncement of celibacy had a significant effect on the development of the Fuji School. It gave rise to nepotism and the hereditary succession of priesthood positions and temple properties within the school. Factions of related priests formed, vying for control. Instead of regarding the spread of the Daishonin's Buddhism as their goal, many priests became increasingly bound by family ties and personal interests.

Celibacy was the norm of Buddhist clergy that helped set them apart from the laity. Priests were known by the Japanese term *shukke,* meaning, "those who have left home," as distinguished from the laity, which was called *zaike,* "those who remain at home." Without remaining celibate, therefore, priests essentially became lay believers who dressed like priests.

Regarding the monastic tradition of celibacy, the Daishonin writes to Sairen-bo as follows:

Now that you have discarded the provisional teachings such as Nembutsu and others and taken faith in the

True Law, you are truly a pure sage among those who uphold the precepts. In any case, when one becomes a priest, even though he is from one of the provisional schools, he should be a priest [who remains celibate and eats no meat]. How much more should this be true of practitioners of the True Law? (GZ, 1357)

On the same subject, the Daishonin states: "Probably because the world has entered into the latter age, even monks who have wives and children have followers, as do priests who eat fish and fowl. I have neither wife nor children, nor do I eat fish or fowl. I have been blamed merely for trying to propagate the Lotus Sutra" (WND, 42). Following his teacher in this regard, Nikko Shonin also states in his "Twenty-six Admonitions": "My disciples should conduct themselves as saintly priests, patterning their behavior after that of the late master" (GZ, 1619). "Saintly priests" indicates those who remain celibate and eat no meat. Judging from these passages, it is clear that the Daishonin and Nikko Shonin viewed celibacy as an essential requisite for those who enter the priesthood and never allowed their priestly followers to disavow that monastic rule.

Regarding the condition of the priesthood at Taiseki-ji after the government decree of 1872, Nichiko Hori, the fifty-ninth high priest, comments that "the recent conduct of priests, which makes them indistinguishable from lay believers," is "a temporary anomaly." He also expressed hope that priestly conduct within Nichiren Shoshu "be restored to the normal state of the period of the founder of the school as well as of the founder of the head temple" (*Detailed Accounts of Nikko Shonin of the Fuji School*, p. 437).

Concerning sexual misconduct by priests, Nikko Shonin

states in his "Twenty-six Admonitions," "However, even if a high priest or a priest striving for practice and understanding should temporarily deviate from sexual abstinence, he should be assigned among the ranks of ordinary priests" (GZ, 1619). Ordinarily, when priests of any Buddhist school were found to have engaged in sexual misconduct, they were expelled from the priesthood and returned to the laity. In this article, however, Nikko Shonin suggests that if the offense constitutes a temporary lapse, those found guilty should be demoted to the rank of ordinary priests. As Nichiko Hori comments on this passage, "There is no other way to interpret [this passage] than as indicating demotion from the eminent position of high priest to that of low rank" (*Detailed Accounts of Nikko Shonin of the Fuji School*, p. 438). It is clear that Nikko Shonin saw the possibility that even a high priest might commit sexual misconduct. Once again this passage completely refutes the idea of the infallibility of the high priest.

Fuji School Merges With Erroneous Nichiren Schools

In September 1872, five months after it issued the decree lifting the ban on priests' marriages, the Meiji government decided to organize Buddhism into seven schools, each of which was to be headed by one chief executive priest. They were: Tendai, True Word, Pure Land, Zen, True Pure Land, Nichiren and Ji schools. Later, however, the Nichiren School was divided into two schools. One held that the essential and theoretical teachings of the Lotus Sutra are equal in merit. It was, therefore, called the Itchi (Oneness) School. The other asserted that the essential teaching is superior to the theoretical teaching and was thus referred to as the Shoretsu (Superior–Inferior) School. In May 1874, Taiseki-ji joined the Shoretsu School of Nichiren Buddhism, which consisted of the Nikko branch, the Myoman-ji branch, the Honjo-ji branch, the Eight-chapter branch and the Honryu-ji branch. The Fuji School headed by Taiseki-ji was considered a sub-branch of the Nikko branch.

In February 1876, Taiseki-ji, Honmon-ji in Kitayama, Yobo-ji in Kyoto, Myoren-ji in Fuji, Kuon-ji in Koizumi, Myohon-ji in Hota, Honmon-ji in Nishiyama and Jitsujo-ji in Izu seceded from the Shoretsu School and formed the Nikko branch of the Nichiren School. The head priests of those eight temples took turns assuming a one-year term as chief executive priest. During this period, Taiseki-ji officially merged with other Nichiren schools and was placed under the jurisdiction of temples whose doctrines it considered to be slanderous of the Daishonin's teaching. Furthermore, when Nippu and Nichio of Taiseki-ji became the chief executive priests of this combined school, they did nothing to refute the errors of the other temples.

Later, the Nikko branch renamed itself the Hon'mon or "True Teaching" School. Although the eight temples of the Nikko branch descended from Nikko Shonin, their historical background and doctrines differed significantly from one another. Hence, the alliance of various Nikko denominations was short-lived. In September 1900, Taiseki-ji's request to become independent of other Nikko branches was granted by the government, and the temple named itself the Fuji branch of the Nichiren School. Later, in June 1912, Taiseki-ji decided that it was inappropriate to call itself a branch of the Nichiren School, which it considered doctrinally deviant. So, following its claim to the orthodoxy of the Daishonin's

Buddhism, a group of temples led by Taiseki-ji renamed itself Nichiren Shoshu or "the true school of Nichiren." In this context, Taiseki-ji's history as Nichiren Shoshu, or an independent school of Nichiren Buddhism, is relatively short.

Taiseki-ji's merger and associations with erroneous Nichiren schools during the late nineteenth and early twentieth centuries were chiefly motivated by concern for its survival. The Fuji School led by Taiseki-ji then was a diminutive sect. According to research conducted in 1904, the Fuji School had eighty-seven temples with only forty-seven chief priests, and approximately fifty-eight thousand parish members. Its relatively small size motivated the head temple administration to seek alliances with larger schools to gain prestige and security.

One consequence of its merger with other Nichiren schools was that, by the beginning of the twentieth century, the Fuji School had grown desensitized to the doctrinal errors of those schools, which were descended from one or another of the five senior priest disciples of the Daishonin or from among the disciples of Nikko Shonin. The Fuji School's disregard for its own doctrinal integrity is particularly apparent in an incident that took place in the early twentieth century concerning the bestowal of an imperial title upon Nichiren Daishonin.

On September 11, 1922, the high priests of various Nichiren schools submitted a petition to the emperor requesting that he bestow the title of "Great Teacher" upon the Daishonin. Nissho, then the fifty-seventh high priest of Taiseki-ji, also signed the petition. In response, the emperor declared that the Daishonin should be called Great Teacher Rissho (The Establishment of the Truth). Eight representatives of the various Nichiren schools who submitted the petition went to the ministry of the imperial household and received the decree. These included the high priest of the Mount Minobu-based Nichiren School, Nichien Isono; the high priest of Nichiren Shoshu, Nissho Abe; and the high priest of the Kempon Hokke School, Nissho Honda. This party of high priests then moved to the Suiko-sha, a clubhouse for high-ranking naval officers. There they recited the "Life Span" chapter of the Lotus Sutra and chanted daimoku, led by Nichien Isono. After reciting the sutra, congratulatory words were exchanged. Nissho, the high priest of Taiseki-ji, delivered a closing speech. After the event, all the high priests posed together for a commemorative photo.

To encourage his future disciples to protect the integrity of the Daishonin's teaching, especially against the erroneous doctrines of the five senior priests, Nikko Shonin wrote in his "Twenty-six Admonitions": "You should not sit together with slanderers of the Law for fear of suffering the same punishment as they" (GZ, 1618). Nissho's action indicates that he was completely oblivious to this admonition from Nikko Shonin. Not only did he seat himself with priests from erroneous Nichiren schools in a religious ceremony, but he recited the sutra and chanted daimoku with them. Although the priesthood at Taiseki-ji called itself Nichiren Shoshu or "the true school of Nichiren," its actions, as this incident indicates, contradicted its claim of orthodoxy.

Nichikan, the twenty-sixth high priest, asserted that Nichiren's honorific title should be "Great Sage" [Jpn Daishonin], for he is the Buddha who revealed Nam-myoho-renge-kyo as the seed of enlightenment for all people of the Latter Day (*Essential Writings of the Fuji School*, vol. 3, p. 306). Furthermore, Nichikan explains that Nichiren called himself a great sage, citing a passage from "A Sage Perceives the Three Existences of Life," which states, "I, Nichiren, am the foremost sage in Jambudvipa" (WND, 642).

Nichikan criticizes those who refer to Nichiren in a way that fails to indicate the importance of his enlightenment. He states: "Why does everyone in the other schools refer to Nichiren as the 'Great Bodhisattva'? This is because of an imperial edict.... They rely on the decree of an emperor of the secular world. But we rely on the decree of the Lord of the Law from the enlightened world" (*Essential Writings of the Fuji School*, vol. 3, pp. 306–07). Here Nichikan refutes those who profess to be followers of Nichiren for basing their understanding of their founder on the interpretation of political authority. Nichikan explains that Nichiren's title *Daishonin* expresses the religious significance of his life. Thus, it must be treated as a doctrinal issue and decided based on his writings, not on secular authority.

Like the title "Great Bodhisattva," the title "Great Teacher" in Japan had been bestowed by the emperor upon founders and eminent priests of various Buddhist schools. For example, Kukai, the founder of the True Word School, received from the emperor the title of Great Teacher Kobo; Shinran, the founder of the True Pure Land School, Great Teacher Kenshin; Honen, the founder of the Pure Land School, Great Teacher Enko; and Dogen, the founder of the Soto branch of the Zen School, Great Teacher Shoyo. To request such a title from political authority on behalf of the Daishonin reflected the ignorance of these priests concerning his identity and his life's work. It was an act contrary to the Daishonin's defiant spirit toward political authority and his commitment to the spiritual freedom and empowerment of the people. High Priest Nissho's acceptance of the imperial title for the Daishonin is testimony to the priesthood's ignorance of its founder's teaching.

Cooperation among various Nichiren schools, as evidenced in their joint petition for the imperial title of "Great Teacher," actively began in the twentieth century. In November 1914, at Ikegami Honmon-ji, a temple of the Minobu Nichiren School, a conference was held to discuss the unification of Nichiren Buddhism. The high priests of various Nichiren schools attended the conference including: the Minobu Nichiren School, the Kenpon Hokke School, the Hon'mon School, the Hon-Myoho-Hokke School, the Hokke School, and the Hon'mon Hokke School. On behalf of Nichiren Shoshu, High Priest Nissho attended the conference, accompanied by Houn Abe, who was later to become the sixtieth high priest, Nichikai, and was also the father of the current high priest Nikken Abe.

Conference participants discussed the unification of the various Nichiren denominations, setting up intercommunication, the establishment of educational institutions and the election of members of a committee to negotiate the process. Making no attempt to point out the errors of the other Nichiren schools, who failed to view the Daishonin as the original Buddha, Nissho joined the conference and posed for a group photo afterward. Nissho and the rest of the priesthood at Taiseki-ji, who looked up to the high priest as a master, grew forgetful of the Daishonin's admonition: "Both teacher and followers will surely fall into the hell of incessant suffering if they see enemies of the Lotus Sutra but disregard them and fail to reproach them" (WND, 747).

At this point, Nichiren Shoshu had distanced itself from the Daishonin's teaching until there was no clear distinction in terms of behavior between Nichiren Shoshu and other Nichiren schools. The unification of Nichiren schools never materialized, but the movement created a momentum leading to the joint petition for the imperial title of "Great Teacher."

Nichiren Shoshu's doctrinal compromise with other Nichiren schools did not end with its petition for the imperial title. In April 1931, Nikki Okada, chief priest of Kuon-ji, the head temple of the Nichiren School at Mount Minobu, submitted a petition to the Ministry of Education, the government agency responsible for religious organizations, requesting that the emperor present Kuon-ji with his calligraphy of the word *Rissho* to commemorate the 650th anniversary of the Daishonin's passing. In response, the ministry asked the Mount Minobu-based Nichiren School to obtain consent from other Nichiren-related schools. A memorandum was circulated among the schools acknowledging that Nichiren's tomb exists at Kuon-ji at Mount Minobu—heads of each school signed the memorandum, thus consenting to the emperor's bestowal of his calligraphy upon the head temple of the Nichiren School at Minobu. Nichikai Abe, the sixtieth high priest of Taiseki-ji, was among those who signed the memorandum.

On October 1, 1931, the emperor's calligraphy was bestowed on Kuon-ji, and it was displayed at a memorial hall on the temple grounds. Based on its claim that Nichiren's tomb exists at Minobu, the Nichiren School attempted to unify the other Nichiren schools around it by taking advantage of imperial authority. Taiseki-ji's acknowledgement of the Daishonin's alleged tomb at Kuon-ji, however, contradicts the intent of Nikko Shonin, who left Mount Minobu with the Dai-Gohonzon and the Daishonin's ashes due to the slanderous acts of the province steward. By yielding to Kuon-ji's claim, Taiseki-ji compromised once again its doctrinal integrity as a school descended from Nikko Shonin.

During the first half of the twentieth century, Taiseki-ji was plagued by fierce factional struggles for the seat of high

Factional Infighting for the Position of High Priest

priest. To resolve disputes over who should succeed to the post, elections were held. But fraudulence and corruption interfered with elections for high priest, eventually prompting government intervention, both by the police and the Ministry of Education.

On August 18, 1923, Nissho, the fifty-seventh high priest, died at Okitsu, Shizuoka Prefecture, where he had been convalescing from an illness. Before his death, however, he did not directly transfer the highest office of Nichiren Shoshu to his successor, Nitchu, grand study master, the position then stipulated by the school's rules to be filled by the candidate for the office of high priest. Instead, Nissho invited two lay believers to Okitsu where he was staying and entrusted them, as temporary custodians, with the heritage of the Law, the formal lineage of the Fuji School. Later these two lay believers transferred the heritage to Nitchu at Renge-ji, a branch temple in Osaka.

The reason behind this unusual method of transferring the office of high priest was that Houn Abe, who later became the sixtieth high priest Nichikai, was trying to interfere with the appointment of Nitchu as the next high priest at all costs. Houn Abe, then leading a faction against Nissho within the priesthood, schemed to keep Nitchu away from Nissho so that the former might not receive the heritage. He also applied various forms of pressure to Nitchu, attempting to force his resignation from the position of grand study master. After his attempt failed and Nitchu became high priest, Houn Abe schemed to force him out of office.

On November 18, 1925, Nichiren Shoshu held a council meeting at Taiseki-ji. Originally, they met to discuss their stance toward the Nichiren School at Mount Minobu. But two days later, the council suddenly passed a resolution calling for the impeachment of Nitchu. Following the resolution, the council issued a recommendation to the high priest that he resign. Prior to their meeting, the majority of council members had entered into a secret agreement to impeach Nitchu, a plan masterminded by Houn Abe.

Abe's scheming was chiefly motivated by his personal grudge against the high priest and his own ambition for the school's highest office. Four months before the council met, Nitchu had demoted Abe from the position of secretary general, as well as from his executive standing within the priesthood, for the errors he had made in an article critical of the Nichiren School at Minobu. Abe's article, published in *Dai-Nichiren*, the priesthood's official magazine, was intended to refute the tenets of the Nichiren School but instead became an object of ridicule in religious circles for its elemental mistakes.

In accord with its plan, the council successfully coerced Nitchu into writing a letter of resignation and reported to the Ministry of Education that the next high priest would be Nichiko Hori. However, leading parish members of Taiseki-ji started to campaign on behalf of the deposed high priest and decided to stop their financial contributions to those priests who supported Nitchu's impeachment. The two factions fought bitterly.

The bureau of religious affairs within the Ministry of Education, which exercised enormous control over religious organizations, saw no possibility of arbitration in the dispute and instructed Nichiren Shoshu to hold an election to determine the high priest. At that time, there were about ninety priests qualified to vote under the school's rules and regulations. On February 17, 1926, ballots were taken. Supported by the leading faction and widely respected for his character and scholarship, Nichiko Hori won a landslide victory. Nitchu received only three out of eighty-seven votes. Before the election, Nitchu declared that he would not transfer the office of high priest to anyone, no matter who was elected. Despite his threat, he received only two votes besides his own.

After the election, however, some parish members lodged a complaint with the local police department that the leading faction, led by Houn Abe, had coerced Nitchu into writing his letter of resignation. Many priests were summoned to the police station for questioning. The turmoil was finally settled on March 8 when Nitchu transferred the high office to Nichiko.

Nichiko, who was more respected for his scholarship and integrity than Abe, had been persuaded by Abe's faction to run against Nitchu. As soon as Nichiko assumed that office, however, Abe began working to isolate Nichiko and force him out.

While in office, High Priest Nichiko tried to revise the school's rules and regulations to eliminate the rampant infighting characteristic of that time. But the committee overseeing the revisions, the council and the staff of the administrative office successfully sabotaged Nichiko's efforts. Lacking any support, Nichiko chose to retire and did so in November 1927, little more than a year after taking office. Upon his retirement, Nichiko expressed his desire to work on a compilation of the complete works of the Daishonin and of the Fuji School. Besides being disappointed at the subterfuge he had faced from other high-ranking priests, Nichiko was also dissatisfied with the contents of what was known as the heritage of the Law—the supposedly secret transmission passed from one high priest to the next— which he had received from Nitchu. After becoming high priest, Nichiko met with the two lay believers who had received the transmission of the heritage from Nissho to reconfirm its contents.

Upon Nichiko's resignation, another election for high priest was held. Two candidates, Houn Abe and Koga Arimoto, ran for the office. The ballots were counted on December 18, 1927, with Abe receiving fifty-one votes, and Arimoto, thirty-eight. Abe had defeated his opponent by a margin of thirteen votes. This election, however, was tainted by corruption. Charges of fraud, including extortion, bribery and obstruction of votes, were brought by Arimoto's supporters. Furthermore, after the election, Abe was investigated by police and charged with embezzlement. He allegedly had cut down trees on the head temple grounds and illegally used the profits from their sale to fund his election campaign.

Because so many allegations were made concerning the election and its results, Nichiren Shoshu had no choice but to seek help from the bureau of religious affairs in the Ministry of Education. In June 1928, after six months of arbitration, the ministry finally acknowledged the election result, and Houn Abe, now called Nichikai, became the sixtieth high priest of Nichiren Shoshu. Meanwhile, the faction led by Koga Arimoto continued to attack Nichikai, accusing him of election fraud, lack of scholarship and sexual misconduct. (Houn Abe, when he was assigned to Josen-ji in Tokyo, had an illicit affair with Suma Hikosaka, a young servant, and had a son out of wedlock. Five years later Abe legally recognized his son. That son, Shinno Abe, went on to become Nikken, the sixty-seventh high priest.) In an open letter dated March 13, 1928, Arimoto's supporters declared that Nichikai's appointment as high priest would be "an ignominy of the priesthood."

The factional infighting in the early 1900s also attracted much attention from the media. The March 16, 1926, edition of the local paper, *Shizuoka Minyu Shimbun*, reports: "Nichiren Shoshu Taiseki-ji continues its ugly infighting. Priests and parish members have abandoned their proud tradition of the transmission of the heritage of the Law handed down from the founder seven hundred years ago and are fighting one another over the election of a high priest, causing public embarrassment to their school."

If what was known as the heritage possessed by the high priest had been sacred and absolute, the factional infighting and elections for the office of high priest would have been regarded as grave sacrilege. In reality, however, many priests did not recognize it as such and thus caused a drawn-out internal conflict over the seat of high priest. This is further evidence from the history of the Fuji School, which makes clear that the doctrine of the infallibility of the high priest is no more than a makeshift dogma. It is a position conveniently invoked by the priesthood to silence criticism toward the high priest.

The corruption within the temple administration spread throughout the priesthood during the nineteenth and twentieth centuries. In the late nineteenth century, some priests who were residents at Taiseki-ji deceived Nippu, the fifty-fifth high priest, and replaced the copper roofing of the Five-Storied Pagoda on the head temple grounds with much cheaper tin roofing. They sold off the expensive original roofing and embezzled the profit, most of which was spent on entertainment.

In April 1941, it was discovered that eight valuable swords had been stolen from the head temple's treasury. One of them was a famous sword that had been forged by the renowned sword-smith Sanjo Kokaji Munechika and given to the Daishonin by Hojo Yagenta. This sword was one of the most treasured articles belonging to the Daishonin kept at Taiseki-ji. It was suspected the theft was an inside job—committed by someone within the priesthood. But the temple administration neither reported the incident to the police nor did it launch an internal investigation. No suspect was identified, and the crime remained an unresolved mystery.

During the seventeenth century, Kyodai-in, an influential patron of Taiseki-ji, cautioned the temple officials in a letter: "Many of the high priests have sold off the treasures [of Taiseki-ji] for their own selfish gain, though some have tried to repair items so that no inconvenience will result from their being damaged" (*Essential Writings of the Fuji School*, vol. 8, p. 59). Despite her warning, misuse and theft of temple property by priests continued well into the twentieth century.

CHAPTER 11

The Priesthood's Wartime Behavior

On December 25, 1926, Japan's Emperor Taisho died. A new emperor, Showa—known to the world outside Japan by his given name, Hirohito—took the throne, and the era was renamed Showa. During the early years of Hirohito's reign, Japan grew increasingly nationalistic, with the military gaining a growing influence in politics. As the nation ran headlong toward war, the Nichiren Shoshu priesthood succumbed to pressure from the government and compromised Nichiren Daishonin's teachings in support of the nation's war efforts and the state-supported Shinto religion, which promoted belief in the divinity of the emperor. The priesthood's behavior contrasted sharply with that of the newly formed Soka Kyoiku Gakkai, whose first and second presidents demonstrated uncompromising commitment to the integrity and spread of the Daishonin's Buddhism. (The Soka Kyoiku Gakkai, or "the educational society for value-creation," was the name of the Soka Gakkai prior to the war and its postwar reconstruction.)

During the 1920s and '30s, Japan's militarist regime

Distortion of the Daishonin's Teachings

109

tightened its control over thought and religion. It cracked down on religious organizations deemed unfavorable to government policy. The Omoto, Hitonomichi and Honmichi sects were disbanded by the government. In 1941, the government revised the Maintenance of the Public Order Act in order to unify all religious organizations under the umbrella of state Shinto. The revised act stipulated "any blasphemous act against the dignity of a Shinto shrine" as punishable with the maximum sentence of death. The act became a pretext for the government to oppress religious organizations, especially newly established groups and Christian denominations.

The government also pressured the various Nichiren schools to delete passages from the Daishonin's writings it viewed as disrespectful toward the emperor and the Shinto deity. In June 1941, the newly merged Nichiren School, which consisted of the Minobu, Kenpon Hokke and Hon'mon schools, decided to delete 208 phrases and passages from about seventy of the Daishonin's writings. The school also discontinued the publication and sale of any of the Daishonin's writings.

Following the lead of the combined Nichiren School, the Nichiren Shoshu administrative office issued a notice, dated August 24, 1941, stating that because the Daishonin's works were written more than seven hundred years ago during the social conditions of the Kamakura period, people of the present age in reading his writings might "doubt the Daishonin's desire to respect the emperor and protect his empire." Thus the priesthood decided to stop publication of the Daishonin's writings.

The notice also states: "The doctrine that the Buddha is true while deities are transient is a vulgar belief in Buddhism. . . . This school, therefore, shall not rely on this doctrine as it has been previously interpreted." Nichiren

Daishonin's Buddhism views the positive and nurturing workings of the environment as "Buddhist deities" and regards them as ephemeral manifestations of the Mystic Law to which Buddhas are enlightened. In this sense, his teaching subordinates "deities" to "Buddhas." Fearing oppression from the government, the priesthood thus abandoned one of the essential teachings of its founder.

Furthermore, on September 29, the Nichiren Shoshu Study Department issued a notice that instructed the deletion of passages from the Daishonin's writings where the nation's sovereignty, symbolized by the Sun Goddess—which Shinto considers to be the supreme deity and origin of Japan's imperial lineage—is described as inferior or subordinate to the Buddha. For example, the priesthood deleted the passage where the Daishonin states, "I, Nichiren, am the foremost sage in Jambudvipa" (WND, 642). Nichikan, the twenty-sixth high priest of Taiseki-ji, who restored the Daishonin's teaching within the Fuji School by correcting erroneous doctrines advocated by his predecessors, considered this passage to be one of those constituting scriptural proof of the Daishonin's identity as the original Buddha. The Fuji School's view of the Daishonin's identity was a doctrinal mainstay that distinguished it from other Nichiren denominations, especially the Minobu School. The notice from the priesthood's Study Department also prohibited the use of the deleted passages in sermons or lectures. The priesthood's decision to delete key passages of the Daishonin's writings and ban their usage was a serious doctrinal compromise.

In addition, Nichiren Shoshu revised the silent prayers of its liturgy to appease the military regime. Published in an August 22, 1941, notice, the new silent prayers extolled the nationalistic ideals of the military regime and promoted state

Shinto. For example, the revised first silent prayer read in part, "I humbly thank the Sun Goddess, the ancestor of the emperor, and all emperors of the successive reigns since the time of first Emperor Jimmu for the great debt of gratitude I owe to them." In the fourth silent prayer, a prayer for the spread of the Daishonin's Buddhism, the priesthood inserted nationalistic expressions such as "the unity of government and people" and "the increase of the nation's majesty."

Behind the priesthood's doctrinal compromise was one high-ranking official of Nichiren Shoshu. Jimon Ogasawara, then a director of propagation, strongly requested that the priesthood adopt the doctrine that the Buddha is subordinate to the Shinto deity. Also, regarding the silent prayers, Ogasawara sharply criticized the head temple administration. In the magazine *Sekai no Nichiren* (Nichiren of the World), he writes: "To place the Sun Goddess after Brahma, Indra and the king devil of the sixth heaven is a great blasphemy. Heavenly deities worshiped in India such as Brahma and Indra must be deleted at once." His criticism was heard, and the Indian deities were promptly deleted from the silent prayers while the Shinto deity and the emperor were given a more prominent place.

Ogasawara's scheme was chiefly motivated by his desire to gain control within the head temple administration. Earlier in his career, he supported Nichikai (father of Nikken; later to become the sixtieth high priest) in order to remove Nitchu, the fifty-eighth high priest, from office. But when Nichikai campaigned for the high office in an election after the resignation of the fifty-ninth high priest, Nichiko, Ogasawara supported his opponent, Koga Arimoto. Nichikai won the election, and Ogasawara lost his influence. Ogasawara was then forced out of the priesthood's ruling faction. By advocating a doctrine that subordinated Buddhism to Shinto, Ogasawara attempted to regain his influence.

Through his close associations with military officials, Ogasawara caused the government to apply pressure on Taiseki-ji. He also sent a letter to High Priest Nikkyo, asking him to clarify his stance regarding the relative merits of the Buddha and the Shinto deity. Ogasawara attempted to lure Nikkyo into making a statement offensive to the military regime, thus placing the high priest in a vulnerable position. Ogasawara's scheme, however, was not successful. He underestimated the priesthood's willingness to compromise its doctrinal integrity to protect itself.

On September 14, 1942, the priesthood expelled Ogasawara, charging him with minor violations of the priesthood's rules and regulations such as failing to pay administrative dues. The decision, however, was political, not doctrinal. The fact that the priesthood continued to support the military regime's nationalistic propaganda based on state Shinto after Ogasawara's expulsion indicates that the head temple administration's decision was motivated by its desire to remove an element hostile to the controlling faction, not by its intent to punish Ogasawara for advocating an erroneous doctrine.

On December 7, 1941, with its surprise attack on Pearl Harbor, Japan declared war against the United States and Great Britain. At the start of the Pacific War, High Priest Nikkyo issued the following message: "Today His Majesty declared war on the United States of America and Great Britain. I can hardly suppress my awe and joy at this.... I ask that all believers summon forth the faith and practice they assiduously developed thus far and ensure victory in this great, unprecedented battle, through their resolve to endure any hardship and exert their utmost in their respective positions and capacities."

As the nation plunged into war, the priesthood's support for the military regime became even more enthusiastic. The January 1942 issue of *Dai-Nichiren*, the priesthood's official magazine, carried Nikkyo's New Year message in which he repeated nationalistic propaganda in support of the nation's war efforts. In this message, Nikkyo declares, "It is the purpose of the founder's advent for us to realize the principle 'the world is the Japanese nation' through loyally dedicating our lives to the nation." On October 10, 1942, one month after Ogasawara's expulsion, the Nichiren Shoshu administrative office issued a notice instructing believers henceforth to face and worship in the direction of the Ise Shinto Shrine at 10:00 a.m. every October 17, when an important annual Shinto harvest festivity was customarily held there.

This act by the priesthood would certainly have been viewed as an abomination by Nikko Shonin, who instructed his disciples as follows: "Lay believers should be strictly prohibited from visiting [heretical] temples and shrines. Moreover, priests should not visit slanderous temples or shrines, which are inhabited by demons, even if only to have a look around. To do so would be a pitiful violation [of the Daishonin's Buddhism]. This is not my own personal view; it wholly derives from the sutras [of Shakyamuni] and the writings [of Nichiren Daishonin]" (GZ, 1617).

On November 19, 1942, the priesthood established the Nichiren Shoshu Association for Serving the Nation (Jpn Nichiren Shoshu Hokokudan) "in order that priests and lay believers in each parish cooperate and unite for the promotion of the movement to serve the nation." The association's chief purpose—to serve the nation—meant to support the national war effort. The association raised money for the war and encouraged its members to pray for Japan's victory as well as for the success and good fortune of the Imperial Army. The high priest became the association's first secretary general.

While the priesthood supported the nation's war efforts, the Soka Kyoiku Gakkai continued to uphold the Daishonin's teachings and refused to accept Shinto. The priesthood grew nervous about the lay organization's stance. In June 1943, the priesthood summoned Gakkai leaders to the head temple. With Nikkyo, the sixty-second high priest, and Nichiko, the retired fifty-ninth high priest, in attendance, Jikai Watanabe, then director of general affairs, instructed Gakkai members to accept a Shinto talisman, a small religious paper depicting the Sun Goddess. The government was urging all households to enshrine and worship this talisman. President Tsunesaburo Makiguchi refused. Later that same month, Makiguchi returned to the head temple to remonstrate with the high priest on this point. His warning, however, fell on deaf ears. Instead of heeding Makiguchi's warning, the priesthood attempted to discipline the Gakkai leaders for their disobedience by barring them from the head temple.

In July, twenty-one Soka Gakkai leaders, including President Makiguchi and General Director Josei Toda, were arrested. Shortly before this crackdown, on June 16, Renjo Fujimoto, a Nichiren Shoshu priest, was arrested for treason. (Fujimoto eventually died in prison in January 1944.) Alarmed by the arrests, the head temple administration expelled Fujimoto from the priesthood and stripped the Gakkai leaders of their status as believers in the school. The priesthood denied all ties with those who, on account of their belief in Nichiren Daishonin's Buddhism, had offended the military regime.

Still Nichiren Shoshu's support for the nation's war efforts and its disciplinary measures against those who disobeyed were not enough to put the minds of Nichiren Shoshu priests at ease. During priests' seminars held at Taiseki-ji on August 21 and 22 and again on August 25 and 26, the head temple administration instructed participants to enshrine a Shinto talisman in their living quarters at their branch temples. On November 1, the head temple's administrative office issued a notice instructing all believers to visit a local Shinto shrine for a Shinto festivity to commemorate the birth of the late Emperor Meiji and to pray for Japan's victory in the war.

The priesthood also contributed head temple properties to the military regime. Giant cedar trees on the temple grounds were felled for lumber, and a large bell was removed for military use. The priesthood's official magazine, *Dai-Nichiren*, reported in 1944:

> The contribution of good timber from our sacred grounds was made so that it may be turned into ships to crush the United States and Great Britain, and this accords with the honest desire of the Buddha to secure the peace of the land through establishing the truth (*rissho ankoku*).... These old cedar trees and the large bell, which have been donated,... shall respectively become a ship to carry the soldiers, supplies and weapons of the Imperial Army and bullets to penetrate the breasts of fierce enemies as intended by the Buddha.

In December 1944, the priesthood made the Grand Lodging Hall on the head temple grounds available for a regiment of the Korean Volunteer Army. Despite its euphemistic name, the "volunteer army" consisted of Koreans brought to Japan as farm laborers from their occupied country, under the command of Japanese military officers. Soon after the regiment came to the head temple, a Shinto talisman was enshrined in the Grand Lodging Hall next to the high priest's living quarters. The enshrinement of a Shinto talisman at the head temple was emblematic of the priesthood's distortion of the Daishonin's Buddhism.

While the priesthood at Taiseki-ji was plagued with corruption and factional infighting in the early 1900s, an important event, though unnoticed at the time,

The Martyrdom of Makiguchi

took place in the history of Nichiren Daishonin's Buddhism. In 1928, Tsunesaburo Makiguchi took faith in the Daishonin's teaching, soon followed by his disciple Jogai Toda, who later renamed himself Josei.

Makiguchi was both an educator in practice and an educational scholar. An elementary-school teacher, he later served as a school principal where he gained experience in school administration. A pioneer of pedagogy in Japan, Makiguchi established a unique theory, which he named "the value-creation educational system." At the core of his educational theory was his philosophical belief that the purpose of life was the pursuit of happiness, which he equated with the creation of value.

In November 1930, with help from his disciple Toda, Makiguchi formed a group of educators dedicated to educational reform based on Nichiren Daishonin's Buddhism. The group was called the Soka Kyoiku Gakkai or "Society of Value-Creation Education." As Makiguchi's understanding of the Daishonin's teachings deepened, the Gakkai gradually broadened its scope from that of an educational reform movement to one aimed at building a peaceful society through the reformation of the individual based on Buddhism.

In 1937, the Gakkai held an inaugural meeting and started conducting activities steadily. Makiguchi himself attended discussion meetings and communicated the Daishonin's Buddhism to a broader audience. As a result, people from walks of life other than education started to join the Gakkai. In 1941, the organization began publication of its newspaper *Kachi Sozo* (Value-creation). By this time, the membership had grown to two thousand.

In 1942, the government ordered the Gakkai to cease publication of its newspaper as Japan plunged further into war and government control of religious organizations became more intensive. Despite this pressure from the government, Makiguchi continued to uphold the Daishonin's teachings. At the same time, he was often critical of the priesthood for its unwillingness to protect the integrity of the Daishonin's Buddhism.

At the fifth general meeting of the Soka Kyoiku Gakkai held in November 1942, Makiguchi said, "The Tendai School during the days of Nichiren Daishonin corresponds to today's Nichiren Shoshu among Nichiren denominations" (*Complete Works of Tsunesaburo Makiguchi*, vol. 10, p. 151). By the thirteenth century, Japan's Tendai School, which had been viewed as an orthodox school based on the Lotus Sutra, descended into esotericism similar to that of the Shingon School. Makiguchi indirectly pointed out that, despite Nichiren Shoshu's claim to the orthodoxy of the Daishonin's Buddhism, its substance had degenerated as it curried favor with the military regime. In the same speech, Makiguchi went

The main hall of Yobo-ji temple in Kyoto. High priests were imported from this Minobu-related sect's temple to Nichiren Shoshu for about a hundred years in the early part of the Edo period.

Nissho, the fifty-seventh high priest of Nichiren Shoshu.

Nichikai, who maneuvered himself into office as the sixtieth high priest of Nichiren Shoshu.

Nitchu, the fifty-eighth high priest, who was ousted by a coup staged by Nichikai, who later became the sixtieth high priest.

Nichiko, Nichiren Shoshu's fifty-ninth high priest, who was instrumental in the publication of the *Gosho Zenshu*, a collection of Nichiren Daishonin's writings.

Nissho (third from right), fifty-seventh high priest, who posed for a commemorative photo with the high priests of other sects.

The nun in the far left in the front row is Suma Hikosaka, whose Buddhist name is Myoshu. She is Nikken's mother. On the far right of the front row is Nichikai, sixtieth high priest of Nichiren Shoshu and Nikken's father.

An advertisement for the Gohonzon made of cloth that Nichiren Shoshu ran in its magazine.

Nichio, the fifty-sixth high priest, who inscribed a "Gohonzon for the victory of the war" (referring to World War II).

A scene from a militaristic grand festival at Yasukuni Shrine.

The front section of Ise Shrine.

The Rendai-ji area in Shimoda on Izu Peninsula where
Mr. Makiguchi conducted introductory meetings.

The Kishi residence where Mr. Makiguchi was arrested (the house burned down in 1953).

Suzaki Road where Mr. Makiguchi walked handcuffed after his arrest.

Shimoda Police Station where Mr. Makiguchi was imprisoned.

Tokyo Prison where Mr. Makiguchi and Mr. Toda were both detained.

The second floor hallway of Tokyo Prison.

Nikkyo, the sixty-second high priest, who died in flames.

Jimon Ogasawara, who advocated the supremacy of Buddhist deities over the compassion and wisdom of the Buddha.

Toyotama Prison, where Josei Toda carried out much of his sentence and from which he was released. This photo was taken in 1982.

Taiseki-ji grounds, as they appeared before Mr. Toda initiated a pilgrimage program to support the destitute school.

The Hokkeko headquarters
building in Tokyo, which was
donated by the Soka Gakkai.

The Hokkeko office in Osaka, which was
also donated by the Soka Gakkai.

Soldiers pay homage to
the Yasukuni Shrine,
which was funded by the
Japanese government.

on: "We must ask who among the existing believers of Nichiren Shoshu is experiencing the three obstacles and four devils" (ibid., p. 152). Makiguchi no doubt made this statement with the following passage from the Daishonin in mind:

> If you propagate it, devils will arise without fail. If they did not, there would be no way of knowing that this is the true teaching. One passage from the same volume reads: "As practice progresses and understanding grows, the three obstacles and four devils emerge in confusing form, vying with one another to interfere . . . . One should neither be influenced nor frightened by them. If one falls under their influence, one will be prevented from practicing the correct teaching." This statement not only applies to me but also is a guide for my followers. Reverently make this teaching your own, and transmit it as an axiom of faith for future generations. (WND, 501)

Clearly his statement was directed toward the priesthood, which was compromising the Daishonin's teachings to avoid government persecution. In this regard, Makiguchi also said: "Those who are instructing others without experiencing persecutions themselves are none other than the jailers of hell leading people to the evil paths."

Inspired by Makiguchi's strict guidance, Gakkai members refused to accept the Shinto talisman promoted by the government. But the Gakkai's uncompromising stance made the priesthood uneasy. As a result, the priesthood summoned Makiguchi and other Gakkai leaders to the head temple and instructed them to accept the Shinto talisman.

As mentioned before, Makiguchi rejected the priesthood's

order. In his essay titled "The History and Conviction of the Soka Gakkai," Josei Toda describes the incident as follows:

> The head temple feared persecution if it supported Mr. Makiguchi's contention that unless they follow the teachings of Nichiren Daishonin and Nikko Shonin, any country, family or individual would experience punishment. It seemed that the head temple was more frightened of the possible persecution it would face from the military if believers did not obediently enshrine the Shinto object of worship.
>
> In June 1943, Soka Gakkai leaders were ordered to the head temple. Jikai Watanabe, on behalf of Nichiren Shoshu, suggested that the Gakkai members receive this Shinto talisman in the meantime and follow the direction of the military for awhile. This suggestion was made with the current and retired high priests on hand as witnesses.
>
> Again, Nikko Shonin states in his "Twenty-six Admonitions" that we should not follow even the high priest if he takes actions that oppose the teachings of true Buddhism. In this spirit, President Makiguchi resolutely rejected the idea of accepting the Shinto talisman and left the head temple. On the way home, he said to me: "What I lament is not that one sect will be ruined but that our nation will perish. I am afraid that the Daishonin is indeed sorrowful about this plight. Isn't this the time to admonish the entire nation? I don't know what the head temple is afraid of." (*Seikyo Times*, June 1991, p. 31)

When Makiguchi and other Gakkai leaders were arrested

on charges of treason and other violations of the Maintenance of Public Order Act in July 1943, Nichiren Shoshu stripped them of their status as lay believers. In the same essay, Toda comments on the reaction of the priesthood as follows:

> We should take to heart the strictness of the Daishonin's golden teachings without fearing authority. President Makiguchi had such vehement spirit. Nevertheless, the warped military government treated him like a criminal, even though he had committed no crime. Twenty-one Soka Gakkai leaders were imprisoned solely because they refused to enshrine talismans of the Sun Goddess. At that time, many believers and priests at the head temple were shocked and at a loss as to what to do. When I heard about this, I was ashamed of them. President Makiguchi, myself and our followers were barred from visiting the head temple, and the whole country criticized our families as being enemies of the nation. Those were very strange days. (ibid., p. 31)

Makiguchi, despite intimidation from the government and inhumane conditions in Japan's wartime prison, upheld his belief to the end. He asserted the correctness of the Daishonin's Buddhism to the interrogating prosecutors. The August 1943 issue of *The Special Police Monthly Report* published some of Makiguchi's responses during the interrogations. When asked about the Gakkai's treatment of the Shinto talisman, Makiguchi responded:

> Nowadays a talisman of the Sun Goddess is enshrined in almost every home. So, above all, I have been encouraging [Gakkai members] to remove them. The

reason for their removal is that if individual members enshrine [the talisman] as an object of devotion, it will confuse their faith in the Gohonzon, thus slandering the Law. Furthermore, to enshrine a talisman of the Sun Goddess at home will instead amount to committing treason for the reason I mentioned before. Needless to say, to visit and offer a prayer at those shrines and temples would be to slander the Law. Since the retribution from slandering the Law is weighty, I have been instructing [Gakkai members] not to visit.

When asked if he thought Japan was an evil society of the Latter Day in light of the Lotus Sutra, Makiguchi responded: "[The Daishonin] states that a nation will experience disasters—such as internal strife, revolution, famine and pestilence—and be led to ruin [if it slanders the Lotus Sutra]. Our past history indicates that we experienced such incidents and similar national disasters. The cause for the current Japan–Sino conflict and the war in greater East Asia lies in the nation's slander of the Law." It should be noted that Makiguchi made these statements at a time when the emperor was considered divine, and war declared under his name as just and sacred. Makiguchi was well aware that his statements violated the Maintenance of Public Order Act, whose maximum sentence was capital punishment.

Emaciated from malnutrition and old age, Makiguchi died in Tokyo Detention Center on November 18, 1944. He was seventy-three. The day before, he had been moved out of solitary confinement. Having refused any help from the guard, he dressed himself and walked to the prison's infirmary. Soon afterward he lay down, fell unconscious and the next morning breathed his last.

Later Toda eulogized Makiguchi: "My mentor gave his life to the Lotus Sutra. As he always quoted the Daishonin, saying that it is a wise man's dishonor to be praised by a fool, he at last was praised by the greatest man of wisdom [Nichiren Daishonin]" (*Complete Works of Josei Toda*, vol. 1, p. 529).

Makiguchi's martyrdom stood in contrast to the high priest's tragic death in a fire at Taiseki-ji on June 17, 1945. Around 10:30 p.m., a fire broke out in a meeting hall of the building that housed the high priest's residence and quickly spread through his living quarters, the adjacent study, the Mutsubo Hall and the Reception Hall. It continued to burn until 4:00 a.m. next day. The fire was caused by a student priest's cigarette.

A gruesome discovery was made in the charred ruins. High Priest Nikkyo was found dead—his lower body trapped in an open hearth located in the temple employees' cafeteria. He was the only one who died in the fire. The high priest had been resting in his quarters directly above the cafeteria. The floor burned through and gave out, and the high priest fell and was trapped in the hearth below.

Several unfortunate coincidences contributed to his death. On the day before the fire, Nikkyo had returned to the head temple from a retreat where he had been convalescing. Obesity combined with illness apparently hindered his escape. During a service at Myoko-ji, a branch temple in Tokyo, in September 1945, Kosei Nakajima, then an acting chief executive of Nichiren Shoshu, spoke about the incident:

In the study, three hundred farming corps members were staying. But for some reason, they were unable to assist in fighting the fire. A fire engine parked in front of the gate was not working. Another fire engine at a [military] tank school in Kamiide was out of gasoline. In Fujinomiya, upon hearing of the fire, an engine was quickly readied for duty. But [the firefighters] received no order from the department chief, who was absent, and so they remained idle. By the time they received a request from the Ueno Police Station and rushed to the fire, it had already spread through the reception hall, and not much could be done. There were so many adverse conditions that I can only say that [the fire] was truly karmic.

Before an assembly of believers, Nakajima also referred to Nikkyo's death as "a compassionate admonishment from the Daishonin." Furthermore, he acknowledged that a student priest caused the fire. Later, however, the priesthood distorted the facts. It announced that the fire was set by Korean Volunteer Army soldiers dissatisfied with Japanese military officers and that the high priest took responsibility for the fire and committed an honorable suicide (from *On Refuting the Counterfeit Dai-Gohonzon Theory* [Jpn *Akusho Ita Honzon Gisaku Ron o Funsaisu*], published by the Nichiren Shoshu Propagation Society in 1956, pp. 92–95).

CHAPTER 12

The Soka Gakkai's Postwar Expansion

On July 3, 1945, Josei Toda was released from the Toshima Penitentiary in Tokyo to find his country burned to ashes, people in utter misery and destitution, and the Soka Gakkai nearly destroyed. Jailed in the same facility as his mentor, Tsunesaburo Makiguchi, Toda read the Lotus Sutra and continued to chant Nam-myoho-renge-kyo in his cell. His study and prayer in prison eventually led him to a profound awakening—an awakening to his mission to spread the Daishonin's Buddhism as a leader of the Bodhisattvas of the Earth. These are the bodhisattvas described in the Lotus Sutra who would become the sutra's devout practitioners long after the passing of Shakyamuni Buddha. Upon his release from prison, Toda was resolved to realize the will of his late mentor, who had died in confinement, and spread the Daishonin's teaching throughout war-torn Japan. He wasted no time in beginning the reconstruction of the Soka Gakkai.

In January 1946, Toda renamed the Soka Kyoiku Gakkai ("Society of Value-Creation Education") the Soka Gakkai ("Society of Value Creation"), indicating his broader vision to promote the Daishonin's Buddhism throughout all aspects of society, beyond its application in education. He soon held discussion meetings and led propagation efforts. In July 1949, he published *The Daibyakurenge*, the Soka Gakkai's monthly study journal. In April 1951, he also began the newspaper, *Seikyo Shimbun*.

Toda was inaugurated the second Soka Gakkai president on May 3, 1951. Approximately 3,080 members signed the petition for Toda's inauguration. They represented the active membership of the Gakkai. In his inaugural speech, Toda made a bold declaration: "While I am alive, I will achieve the propagation of 750,000 households by my own hand. If this cannot be achieved in my lifetime, please do not hold my funeral. Just dispose of my body off the coast of Shinagawa" (*Complete Works of Josei Toda*, vol. 3, p. 433).

With Toda's inauguration, the Soka Gakkai launched full-fledged activities to spread the Daishonin's Buddhism. Many people began taking faith in the Daishonin's Buddhism each year. By the end of 1951, the membership had grown to 5,700 households; by the end of 1952, to 22,000 households; in 1953, to 70,000 households; in 1954, to 170,000 households; and by the end of 1955, to 300,000.

Envisioning a dramatic increase in membership, Josei Toda submitted a request to Nissho, the sixty-fourth high priest, to transcribe a Gohonzon for the wide propagation of the Daishonin's Buddhism. In response, the high priest transcribed a Gohonzon with the inscription, "For the achievement of the wide spread of the Great Law through compassionate propagation" and conferred it upon the Soka Gakkai on May 20, 1951. This Gohonzon is symbolic of the Gakkai's essential role, its dedication to broadly disseminating the essence of Buddhism.

The Nichiren Shoshu temples sustained significant damage during the war: The head temple burnt down, and many branch temples were destroyed in air raids. Furthermore, in December 1945, Taiseki-ji lost its farmland in the postwar agrarian reform, which the government was promoting as part of the nation's democratization. The landowners who rented out their land to tenant farmers instead of farming themselves had to sell off their farmland to the government at a fixed price. The government in turn sold those tracts of farmland to tenant farmers. This agrarian reform was instituted between 1946 and 1948. As a result, Japan's land-holding gentry class was virtually eliminated, and the lives of tenant farmers were much improved.

Taiseki-ji had owned a vast tract of farmland donated by its patrons, which it had rented out to farmers for hundreds of bushels of rice per year. The head temple had long depended on the income from this farmland for its operation. So when it lost that farmland in the postwar agrarian reform, the priesthood faced severe financial hardship. The chief priests of the lodging temples on the head temple grounds had to cultivate empty lots and hillsides themselves for meager crops—just enough to keep them from starvation. They did not have enough money even to buy candles for the altars. In this dire financial situation, the Nichiren Shoshu priesthood appealed desperately to its parishioners for more financial support.

In November 1950, the priesthood decided to promote Taiseki-ji as a tourist attraction to generate additional income and held a conference at the reception hall to discuss how. Besides representatives of the priesthood, the mayor of Fujinomiya, the chief of Ueno Village, executives of Fujinomiya's tourist association and local news reporters attended the conference.

During the conference, participants discussed concrete

plans to promote tourism at Taiseki-ji. For example, a scenic road, a tourist information center at the head temple's San-mon Gate and a new lodging facility were suggested. It was also proposed that Taiseki-ji hold a dance to attract young people in the spring and autumn.

During the war, the priesthood curried favor with the military regime and compromised the Daishonin's teaching as part of its wartime strategy to survive. And it nearly led to ruin. The priesthood's plan to promote the head temple as a tourist attraction, however, tells us that it learned little about the importance of upholding the integrity of Buddhism from its wartime experience.

Toda was enraged to hear the priesthood's plan, stating that tourists who were not seeking the Gohonzon must not be allowed on the head temple grounds. His strong opposition prevented the plan from being realized. To relieve the head temple of its financial burden, Toda organized group pilgrimages of Gakkai members. This was in spite of the fact that the number of Gakkai members at the time was relatively small, and their financial prospects were no more hopeful than that of the priesthood.

Toda often expressed his belief that when the True Law is about to be obscured and driven to extinction, that is precisely the time for its true development and broad propagation to begin. Toward 1952, which marked the beginning of the seven-hundredth year since the Daishonin established his Buddhism in 1253, Toda emphasized the necessity of spreading the Daishonin's Buddhism and urged Gakkai members to awaken to their mission as the Bodhisattvas of the Earth.

The celebration to commemorate the establishment of the Daishonin's Buddhism was held at Taiseki-ji on April 27 and

The Ogasawara Incident

28, 1952. Attended by four thousand Gakkai members, the event was unprecedented in scale for both the priesthood and the Gakkai at that time. On April 24, the Soka Gakkai published *The Collected Writings of Nichiren Daishonin* (Jpn Nichiren Daishonin Gosho Zenshu), which had been edited by Nichiko Hori, the retired fifty-ninth high priest and renowned historian of Nichiren Daishonin's Buddhism.

The publication of the Daishonin's writings marked the beginning of the Gakkai's broad-based study movement, solidifying the Gakkai's philosophical foundation. In his preface to *The Collected Writings*, Toda compares Buddhist study to the strict discipline of swordsmanship (GZ, 1). Toda was passionate about the importance of Buddhist study in one's practice.

On the evening of April 27, during commemorative activities at the head temple, Soka Gakkai youth division members found out that Jimon Ogasawara was also staying at the head temple. During World War II, Ogasawara had propounded the erroneous doctrine that regarded the Buddha as a transient manifestation of the Shinto goddess in order to curry favor with the Japan's militaristic regime. He also worked to induce the government to persecute the Gakkai, leading to the imprisonment of Makiguchi and Toda. Ogasawara's presence at the head temple on this auspicious occasion came as a great surprise to the youth division members because he had been long expelled from the priesthood (see chapter 11 for more details).

The youth division members met Ogasawara at one of the lodging temples on the head temple grounds and refuted his erroneous doctrine. Then they escorted him to the grave of

Makiguchi where he wrote a letter of apology to the Daishonin for distorting the Daishonin's teachings. This is known as the Ogasawara Incident.

During the war, Ogasawara pushed for the merger of Nichiren Shoshu and the Minobu-based Nichiren School. He was said to have had a secret agreement with the Nichiren School that allegedly promised him the position of general administrator or the chief priest position at Taiseki-ji or Seicho-ji. Furthermore, Ogasawara attempted to have High Priest Nikkyo arrested on the charge of treason. Ironically, Ogasawara's attempt to take control of the head temple encouraged the Nichiren Shoshu priesthood to stray further from the Daishonin's Buddhism and support Shintoism and the government's war efforts. Since Ogasawara corrupted the Daishonin's Buddhism, incited persecutions against the Soka Gakkai, and attempted to control the head temple for personal gain, he should have been condemned as an enemy not only to the Daishonin's Buddhism and the Gakkai but also to the priesthood.

When youth division members reprimanded Ogasawara's offenses at the head temple, however, the priesthood was not pleased. Though it was a sincere action to protect the integrity of the Daishonin's Buddhism, the head temple administration regarded the incident as a disruption of an auspicious celebration. It also viewed the Gakkai's refutation of Ogasawara as challenging the high priest's prerogative to decide what is orthodox and what is heretical. The Nichiren Shoshu executive priests thought it was inappropriate for lay believers to refute any priest who had been ordained under the high priest's authority. Put simply, the incident was viewed as arrogance by lay believers toward the authority of the priesthood as well as the high priest.

Many priests throughout Japan expressed their discontent.

For example, the chief priest of the Osaka parish issued a letter of protest against the Soka Gakkai on May 13, condemning its action as "an insult to the entire priesthood." The parish of the Kyushu area passed a resolution on May 21 calling for disciplinary action to be taken against the Soka Gakkai. While the priesthood never publicly condemned Ogasawara for his wartime behavior, it severely attacked the Soka Gakkai's action as an insult to the priesthood. The priesthood's emotional reaction to the Ogasawara Incident clearly reflected its deep-seated insecurity and need to maintain a sense of superiority and control over the laity.

In the middle of May, following the incident, the priesthood published the April issue of *Dai-Nichiren*, its official monthly magazine. This belated April issue contained notice of Ogasawara's reinstatement, as of April 5, into the priesthood. In other words, the priesthood retroactively re-admitted Ogasawara to the priesthood after the incident. This provided a pretext for accusing the Soka Gakkai of criticizing a Nichiren Shoshu priest on the head temple grounds.

Actually Ogasawara was reinstated into the priesthood soon after the war. On March 31, 1946, Nichiman, the sixty-third high priest, restored Ogasawara's status as a Nichiren Shoshu priest. His reinstatement was public knowledge within the priesthood as he ran for a position on the Nichiren Shoshu council in 1947. According to an April 28, 1947, publication, Ogasawara was not elected. However, when the Soka Gakkai inquired about Ogasawara's status, the priesthood on numerous occasions denied that he was a Nichiren Shoshu priest. For example, the May 1951 issue of *Dai-Nichiren* contains the following notice from the Nichiren Shoshu administrative office: "The *Seikyo Shimbun* reported that a priest who had filed a suit against High Priest Nikkyo

Suzuki and attempted to disband Nichiren Shoshu still remains at the head temple. It must be clarified, however, that there is no such priest among the Nichiren Shoshu priesthood." So naturally, when the incident took place, none of the Soka Gakkai members suspected that Ogasawara was a Nichiren Shoshu priest.

On June 28, 1952, the Nichiren Shoshu council met to discuss the Ogasawara Incident. The council passed a resolution calling on Toda to submit a letter of apology to the head temple through the chief priest of the branch temple to which he belonged, ordered his dismissal from the position of chief lay representative, and barred him from visiting the head temple.

Outraged by this resolution, the Soka Gakkai youth division visited the council members one by one and tried to convince them of the unjust nature of their decision. Through their efforts, the situation gradually improved. On July 24, Nissho, the sixty-fourth high priest, issued a written admonition to Toda. In response, Toda submitted a letter of apology, in which he expressed his confidence in the action taken by the youth division. He states in the letter: "When we see those in our school who are weak in their faith in the Great Pure Law and leaning toward slander of the Law, because we keep the teachings of Nichiren Daishonin and Nikko Shonin deep in our hearts . . . we tend to be uncompromising in our battle. . . . Since I believe that our action did not contradict the golden words of the Daishonin and Nikko Shonin in the slightest, I am not ashamed to call myself a believer of Nichiren Shoshu before the Gohonzon. Therefore, I will not resign from the position of chief lay representative."

Later Ogasawara lodged a complaint with police against Soka Gakkai leaders, including Toda, and a police investigation of the incident followed. However, Ogasawara filed a complaint also against the high priest, and as a result he was strongly criticized within Nichiren Shoshu. Eventually he retracted his complaints. Even after he caused so much turmoil, the priesthood took no disciplinary action against Ogasawara.

The Ogasawara Incident highlighted the priesthood's desire to protect its authority, as well as its tendency to look condescendingly upon lay believers. Instead of making the Daishonin's teachings a guideline for its behavior, the priesthood allowed its decisions to be driven by these baser motives. In addition, the priesthood was afraid that if it allowed the Gakkai to rebuke Ogasawara for his actions during the war, it would be subjected to the same criticism due to its wartime support of Shintoism and the military regime. In short, the priesthood wanted to protect itself against any possible criticism from the laity.

This incident, however, did not in the least shake the Gakkai's confidence in the Daishonin's teaching or its movement to spread it. When Toda heard about the council resolution to prohibit him from visiting the head temple, he said: "It is all right if they want to bar me from visiting the head temple. It is not as if we cannot attain enlightenment unless we go to the head temple. The Daishonin's writings clearly explain this principle."

In August 1952, the Soka Gakkai was incorporated as an independent religious organization. Toda was keenly aware of the priesthood's authoritarianism and its limitations in terms of its ability and sense of responsibility for the spread of the Daishonin's Buddhism. With incorporation, the Soka

Propagation Led by Josei Toda

Gakkai's propagation efforts made further progress as it could now take the initiative and full responsibility for its actions.

Although the Gakkai strove to spread the Daishonin's Buddhism, the priesthood was not cooperative. Most Nichiren Shoshu priests did not understand the Gakkai's earnest efforts in propagation. Many were even critical. In those early days of the Soka Gakkai's development, there were about one hundred branch temples throughout Japan and ten in Tokyo. Only two temples in Tokyo were willing to conduct initiation ceremonies for new converts introduced by Soka Gakkai members. As the Gakkai conducted its propagation nationwide, more branch temples gradually started to conduct initiation ceremonies.

Because there were virtually no new converts before the existence of the Soka Gakkai, Nichiren Shoshu priests were not accustomed to conducting initiation ceremonies. (Most parishioners and their families had belonged to Nichiren Shoshu temples for generations, and as such, had been considered believers from birth.) As more people took faith in the Daishonin's Buddhism, President Makiguchi saw practical merit in a solemn ceremony to encourage converts in their new faith and draw a distinction between the Daishonin's Buddhism and their previous religious affiliation.

In the Daishonin's Buddhism, however, embracing the Gohonzon in and of itself is to accept the supreme Buddhist precept, so a ceremony was not strictly necessary. When the Daishonin's Buddhism spread rapidly after the war due to the Gakkai's efforts, not many priests knew how to conduct initiation ceremonies, and sometimes Gakkai leaders had to assist priests in doing so.

New members were encouraged by their Soka Gakkai sponsors to remove objects of other Buddhist beliefs so that they might not be confused about their fundamental object of devotion, which is the Gohonzon. The priesthood, however, remained lax in this area. For example, some lodging temples on the head temple grounds continued to enshrine the Shinto talisman even after the Gakkai's organized pilgrimages had begun. As late as the mid-1950s, Soka Gakkai youth division members encouraged one lodging temple to remove a Shinto talisman.

Inspired by Soka Gakkai members, some priests removed objects of other faiths from their temples. For example, in 1953, the chief priest of Myofuku-ji in Fukushima Prefecture removed various Buddhist statues that had been kept at the temple for the previous six hundred years. The temple members, whose families had belonged to the parish for many generations, however, fiercely opposed the removal of those religious objects. On the nights of April 18 and 19, 1953, a mob of disgruntled temple believers stormed the temple, throwing stones and vandalizing the grounds. The police were called, and criminal charges were filed. Later, twenty-two temple members were expelled from Nichiren Shoshu.

Like Myofuku-ji, many branch temples, especially those in northeastern Japan, had kept religious objects from other Buddhist sects for centuries. Also, many temple believers living in the vicinity of the head temple enshrined the objects of other faiths and thus drew Gakkai members' attention. But the priesthood took no significant action regarding this.

Although the head temple professed strict adherence to the Daishonin's and Nikko Shonin's teachings in matters of Buddhist doctrine, it continued to allow its branch temples and parishioners to enshrine objects of other faiths. In this regard, Nichiko Hori, the fifty-ninth high priest, states: "Those who appear to be strict with regard to the slander of the Law yet are lenient in reality are monstrous" (*Essential Writings of the Fuji School,* vol. 1, p. 153).

While the Soka Gakkai continued to spread the Daishonin's Buddhism, it also began making many contributions to the priesthood. On the head temple grounds, Gakkai members' financial contributions made possible the restoration of the Five-Storied Pagoda, the repair of the Somon Gate, the construction of Hoan-den, the construction and renovation of lodging temples, the construction of the Grand Lecture Hall, and so on.

Furthermore, numerous branch temples were constructed and donated by the Gakkai. With the rapid progress of propagation, the priesthood soon attained an unprecedented level of prosperity. The postwar restoration of the priesthood was made possible solely through the Soka Gakkai's efforts. In this regard, Nichiko Hori once said to Toda: "Mr. Toda, if it weren't for you, Nichiren Shoshu would have already collapsed."

With the advent of the Soka Gakkai and its rapid development after World War II, a new era of the Daishonin's Buddhism was unfolding. On New Year's Day in 1956, Nichijun, the sixty-fifth high priest, stated: "When I look back over the last seven hundred years and compare them with our circumstances today, it is apparent that we have undergone a great transformation; a new era in history has been created. That is, through the propagation of the Soka Gakkai, the True Law has spread throughout the nation. The unprecedented expansion of our order is being realized. In this regard, future historians will probably define the first seven hundred years [since the Daishonin's establishment of his Buddhism] as an era of protection by the priesthood, and the era thereafter as an era of spread and propagation"

(*CompleteWorks of High Priest Nichijun*, p. 1620).

Nichijun continues: "Seven hundred years after the Daishonin's establishment of his Buddhism, wide-scale propagation began. The current propagation of the True Law seems to hold profound promise. In this regard, I sense something extraordinary about the Soka Gakkai's appearance, about its relationship with the Buddha" (ibid., p. 1622).

Nichijun realized that the priesthood's role to preserve the Daishonin's teaching was ending, and the Soka Gakkai's era of propagation had begun. Nichijun stated at the seventh Soka Gakkai general meeting on December 7, 1952: "I entrust the great propagation of the Law to the members of the Soka Gakkai" (ibid., p. 308). This statement, leaving the spread of the Daishonin's teachings to Gakkai members, apparently arose from Nichijun's awareness of the priesthood's lack of ability in spreading Buddhism on its own.

On March 11, 1955, the Soka Gakkai held an official debate with the Minobu-based Nichiren School in Otaru, Hokkaido. Instructed by Toda, the Gakkai representatives completely refuted the Minobu Nichiren School's distortions of the Daishonin's Buddhism. While the priesthood was unable to represent itself in debate, the Gakkai clearly validated the correct teaching of the Daishonin through its grasp of Buddhist teachings.

On September 8, 1957, during a youth division athletic meet in Yokohama, Toda made a historic declaration against the use of nuclear weapons, urging the young people present to communicate the Daishonin's emphasis on the respect for life and thus bring lasting peace to the entire world. With his antinuclear declaration, Toda laid the philosophical foundation for the SGI's movement to promote peace and culture based on Buddhism.

By the end of 1957, the Gakkai's membership grew to more than 760,000 households, surpassing Toda's lifelong goal of 750,000 households and thereby solidifying the foundation of the spread of the Daishonin's Buddhism in Japan. His goal complete, Toda died on April 2, 1958. He was fifty-eight. At the eighteenth Soka Gakkai general meeting held soon after Toda's death, on May 3, 1958, High Priest Nichijun stated: "In the Lotus Sutra, great bodhisattvas equal in number to the grains of sand of sixty-thousand Ganges rivers, led by four leaders including the foremost, Bodhisattva Superior Practices, gather at the assembly of Eagle Peak and pledge to spread Myoho-renge-kyo in the Latter Day of the Law. Those bodhisattvas are now appearing as they promised at the assembly on Eagle Peak.

"It was President Toda who, as their leader, called forth those bodhisattvas; it was in the Soka Gakkai that they gathered. In other words, it was President Toda who manifested the five and seven characters of Myoho-renge-kyo as 750,000 [bodhisattvas]" (*Complete Works of High Priest Nichijun*, p. 357). As Nichijun eulogized, Toda, inheriting the will of his mentor, Makiguchi, had reconstructed the Soka Gakkai and laid the foundation for the spread of the Law in Japan in accord with the teachings of the Daishonin and Nikko Shonin.

CHAPTER 13

The Second Phase of Kosen-rufu and the Temple Issue

When Josei Toda died in 1958, many critics in the Japanese media were confident that the Soka Gakkai would not survive without his leadership. Instead, the Gakkai remained united under the leadership of Daisaku Ikeda, who was then chief of staff. On May 3, 1960, he became the third president of the Soka Gakkai.

Daisaku Ikeda's Global Leadership

Inheriting his mentor's will to spread Nichiren Daishonin's Buddhism both far and wide, President Ikeda brought about unprecedented growth on a global scale. In October 1960, soon after his inauguration, he visited North and South America. The following year he traveled to India, accompanied by Nittatsu, the sixty-sixth high priest. Ikeda traveled around the globe—to the Americas, Europe and Asia, including China and the former Soviet Union. Through those visits, he encouraged and nurtured the faith of those living outside Japan while promoting peace, culture and education based on the Daishonin's Buddhism. By 1997 he had visited fifty-four nations.

In January 1975, the First International Buddhist League World Peace Conference was held in Guam. On that occasion, what later was named the Soka Gakkai International was formed, and Ikeda became its first president. Under his leadership the SGI continued to develop. As of 1997, about 1,360,000 members were practicing the Daishonin's Buddhism in 128 countries and territories outside Japan, contributing to their respective communities and nations.

In his writings, the Daishonin expresses his hope for the global spread of his teachings. For example, he states in "On the Buddha's Prophecy": "[The votary of the Lotus Sutra will establish and] spread abroad widely throughout Jambudvipa the object of devotion of the essential teaching, or the five characters of Myoho-renge-kyo" (WND, 400). He goes on to state: "The moon appears in the west and sheds its light eastward, but the sun rises in the east and casts its rays to the west. The same is true of Buddhism. It spread from west to east in the Former and Middle Days of the Law, but will travel from east to west in the Latter Day" (WND, 401). Here the Daishonin indicates that his teaching, which he compares to the sun, will spread from Japan to the rest of the world and save all humanity in the Latter Day.

The Daishonin's vision has been realized through the dedicated efforts of SGI President Ikeda and his fellow SGI members. When the SGI was formed, Nittatsu stated: "The propagation of Buddhism depends on the time. But the time for propagation will not come by itself. It is President Ikeda who has made this the right time for the worldwide growth of true Buddhism. I am certain that Nichiren Daishonin would praise the great accomplishment and tireless dedication of President Ikeda" (March 1975 *Seikyo Times*, p. 15).

While spreading the Daishonin's Buddhism, Ikeda and the Soka Gakkai continued to support the Nichiren Shoshu priesthood. In April 1964, the Soka Gakkai donated to the head temple the Grand Reception Hall, which was built with the finest materials from around the world. On that occasion, the priesthood appointed Mr. Ikeda as chief representative of all Nichiren Shoshu lay believers. Every year the Gakkai built and donated branch temples. Also more lodging temples were built on the head temple grounds by the Gakkai. And, as the membership outside Japan increased, the Gakkai donated branch temples in the United States and Brazil.

Construction of the Grand Main Temple

In October 1972, the Grand Main Temple was completed and donated to the head temple to house the Dai-Gohonzon. The cost of this construction project was financed by more than eight million Gakkai members. At the October 1 completion ceremony, Ikeda elaborated on its purpose: "The Grand Main Temple has been built through the passionate sincerity of more than eight million people. Put simply, this is not an edifice symbolic of religious authority but a facility for the people. . . . This Grand Main Temple is a building in which to pray for the lasting peace of humanity and for the sound progress and development of global culture. Such prayer will be offered by all those who visit here; that is, men and women of all ages and ethnic backgrounds. This is the most prominent feature [of the Grand Main Temple]." Here Ikeda explains that the Grand Main Temple was built for the peace of all humanity, transcending the narrow sectarian concern of prosperity for only Nichiren Shoshu.

Nittatsu, in his "Admonition" dated April 28, 1972, explains the significance of the Grand Main Temple as "the actual high sanctuary of this time" and "the supreme edifice that shall be the high sanctuary of the temple of true Buddhism at the dawn of kosen-rufu." He clarified that when the Daishonin's Buddhism is spread widely in accordance with the Daishonin's will, Taiseki-ji would be renamed Honmon-ji (Temple of the True Teaching), and the Grand Main Temple would become the high sanctuary of that temple, the temple of true Buddhism (i.e., the actual high sanctuary). In a certificate of appreciation presented on October 12, 1972, to Ikeda, who chaired the construction committee, Nittatsu praises his contribution, calling the construction "unprecedented in the school's history and an immortal monument to be exalted by the entire priesthood."

While the Grand Main Temple was being built, one parish group called Myoshinko, which belonged to Hodo-in, a temple in Tokyo, vehemently opposed the construction. They claimed that the high sanctuary must be built only by the sovereign or national government. The idea of a "national high sanctuary" was originally propounded by Chigaku Tanaka (1861–1939), who founded an ultranationalistic lay Nichiren Buddhist group called Rissho Ankoku Kai (Society for Securing the Peace of the Land Through the Establishment of True Buddhism) in 1885. He renamed his group the Kokuchukai (Pillar of the Nation Society) in 1914. During the early 1900s, he promoted the idea of a national high sanctuary.

The Nichiren Shoshu priesthood had also used the term *national high sanctuary*. The expression, however, was deemed inappropriate because the scope of the Daishonin's teaching should not be confined within one nation and the expression often invited criticism that Nichiren Shoshu and the Soka Gakkai were aiming to establish a state religion. So, at the thirty-third Soka Gakkai Headquarters general meeting on May 3, 1970, Nittatsu announced: "From now on, there shall be no use of such terminology [as the national high sanctuary] in this school" (*Seikyo Shimbun*, May 4, 1970).

The Myoshinko, however, insisted on the idea of a national high sanctuary and criticized the priesthood and the Gakkai for rejecting the term. After failing to persuade the group to change its stance, Nittatsu expelled them from Nichiren Shoshu in 1974. On October 4 of the same year, about one hundred youth, members of the Myoshinko, demonstrated in front of the Soka Gakkai Headquarters in Tokyo. Using car-mounted loudspeakers, they demanded a meeting with Hiroshi Hojo, then the general director. Several dozen demonstrators forced their way into the building. Soka Gakkai staff and police officers pushed the demonstrators out of the building and closed the gate to the property.

The demonstrators, however, drove a car through the gate and forced their way into the building once again, injuring more than a dozen Gakkai staff members and vandalizing the facility. The demonstrators were arrested by riot police who had responded to the scene. The Gakkai lodged a criminal complaint against the demonstrators for trespassing, assault, vandalism and other acts, leading to the conviction of three Myoshinko leaders. Later the Myoshinko renamed itself the Kenshokai, and today it is an independently incorporated religious organization. Recently, the Kenshokai has been criticized for aggressive and sometimes violent proselytizing methods that target minors.

Since the Grand Main Temple symbolized the Soka Gakkai's contribution, it later became an object of resentment for the priesthood as animosity toward the Gakkai grew within its ranks. In January 1991, Nikken, the sixty-seventh high priest, disputed the significance of the Grand Main Temple as defined by his predecessor, Nittatsu. Eventually, in April 1998, he removed the Dai-Gohonzon from the Grand Main Temple and announced his plan to demolish the structure. Nikken proclaimed that he would destroy the building "to completely refute the great slander of Ikeda and others."

Many issues arose between the priesthood and the Soka Gakkai during the 1970s. These were, for the most part, rooted in the priesthood's fundamental mistrust of the Soka Gakkai and its deep-seated insecurity about its role and purpose. This was greatly complicated and aggravated by the machinations of a single person, Masatomo Yamazaki, then chief legal counsel for the Soka Gakkai.

Issues Between the Priesthood and the Gakkai in the 1970s

Seen from another perspective, the Gakkai's progressive ideals and openness to society, which had become more apparent in the 1970s, caused a backlash within a priesthood constrained by its conservative traditions and institutional authoritarianism. The temple's inability to understand and embrace the breadth and depth of the Gakkai's movement led to deep frustration among priests, which was born out in repressive action.

After the Grand Main Temple was completed in 1972, the Gakkai began conducting its activities and spreading the Daishonin's Buddhism in a broader and more flexible manner than it had during its period of rapid growth during the fifties and sixties.

This new phase of development was referred to as "the second chapter of kosen-rufu." In his speech delivered on November 2, 1972, Ikeda remarked: "We now greet a new sunrise. It is the dawn of the second chapter of kosen-rufu, a voyage toward realization of true global peace" (January 1973 *Seikyo Times*, p. 13). In this new phase, the Gakkai began communicating the Daishonin's teaching as a philosophy that elucidates the profound workings and potential of human life.

Later in the same speech, Ikeda stressed this very point: "It is not too much to say that the Soka Gakkai begins and ends with the philosophy of life. To be more specific, the Soka Gakkai has as its essential foundation the enlightenment that Mr. Toda attained in prison. The theory of life, however, is not one formulated by the Gakkai organization. Nichiren Daishonin's Buddhism is in itself the philosophy of life that the Soka Gakkai inherited in its purest form. Thus the kernel of the Soka Gakkai's teaching lies in Nichiren Daishonin's writings and in the enlightenment of Mr. Toda who interpreted these documents as revealing the philosophy of life" (ibid., pp. 15–16).

The priesthood could not appreciate the fact that lay believers were now gaining a sufficiently profound grasp of Buddhist principles to interpret the writings of Nichiren Daishonin on their own, without clerical instruction, thus successfully convincing many others of the greatness of the Daishonin's Buddhism. The priesthood's inability to explain Buddhism to a broad and diverse audience and its diminishing role in guiding lay believers exacerbated the priests' insecurity. This greatly contributed to friction with the Gakkai in the 1970s.

Furthermore, after the completion of the Grand Main Temple in 1972, the Gakkai, with Nittatsu's approval, began to build more community centers. Until that time, the Gakkai's resources had been mainly devoted to the development of the head temple and its branch temples. Besides building the Grand Main Temple and many branch temples, the Gakkai donated the following buildings to the head temple grounds: the Daikejo Hall in 1960, the Daibo Hall in 1962, the Grand Reception Hall in 1964, the Mutsubo Hall in 1965 and the Tenrei-in Hall in 1969, not to mention many lodging facilities.

Conversely, during this time, the Gakkai's rapidly growing membership suffered from a shortage of adequate facilities for its own use. While the Gakkai's desire to build more centers for the benefit of its members was understandable, the organization nonetheless never stopped building temples for the priesthood. Rather, it simply shifted its emphasis from funneling nearly all of its available resources to the priesthood to dedicating a portion of those resources to building community centers and related facilities. Young priests who had not yet been assigned to their own branch temples were not pleased by this decision. They were concerned about their financial prospects and felt that they were being deprived of the prosperity and comfort that should have been afforded them by the lay organization. These young priests, who had been ordained under Nittatsu, later formed a core of anti-Soka Gakkai sentiment within the priesthood.

The Gakkai also started to improve its organizational structure and procedures, especially in terms of legal and administrative aspects. The Gakkai's efforts to improve itself as a religious corporation made many priests apprehensive, and some concluded that the Gakkai was preparing to separate itself from the priesthood. Furthermore, the priesthood had become completely dependent upon the Gakkai. Their resulting sense of insecurity led them to misinterpret the Gakkai's sincere intentions at every juncture during the mid to later 1970s.

Keenly aware of this atmosphere of mistrust, the lawyer Yamazaki took steps to aggravate the situation with his personal gain in mind. An understanding of Yamazaki's role in manipulating the priesthood is essential to gaining insight into the problems that occurred between the priesthood and the Soka Gakkai in the 1970s and, more important, into the fundamental nature of the priesthood itself. It also sheds light on the enormous influence of the media on people's perception of a religious movement that seeks to establish deep roots into society.

For the first time in its history, the Soka Gakkai experienced extensive, ongoing media attacks, most of which were concentrated on Ikeda himself. Yamazaki cleverly took advantage of this media influence and used it to undermine the spread of the Daishonin's Buddhism. In this sense, the temple issue during the 1970s was a painful yet valuable experience for the Gakkai in terms of promoting its Buddhist movement in an increasingly information-oriented society. (For a more detailed explanation of what took place in the 1970s, please refer to the timeline in Appendix A.)

Yamazaki became legal counsel for the Soka Gakkai in May 1970. In dealing with issues regarding the Myoshinko, Yamazaki developed close contacts with the Nichiren Shoshu administration. He saw an opportunity to amass wealth through his actions as an intermediary between the priesthood and the Gakkai. Yamazaki started to manipulate the tension between both parties. Throughout most of the late 1970s, he fueled the priesthood's antagonism toward the Gakkai by feeding it misinformation.

Yamazaki's greed and corruption may be summed up in his view of the Soka Gakkai as a moneymaking opportunity. For example, in 1975, Yamazaki earned a handsome profit from a real estate deal involving the priesthood and the Gakkai. He persuaded Taiseki-ji to sell a large tract of land in Fujinomiya City to his own paper company at a low price. Yamazaki then sold the property to a developer who, in turn, sold it to the Gakkai for a cemetery park.

Each time the land was bought and sold, the price was inflated. From this real estate deal, Yamazaki amassed a profit of some 50 million yen, which he did not properly report as income. When the Gakkai bought another property for a memorial park from the same developer, Yamazaki received a kickback of about 400 million yen from the developer for arranging that an affiliate company be involved in the construction.

By leaking misinformation to the priesthood, he also aroused its distrust of the Gakkai and then contrived to position himself as a mediator to resolve the conflict. In the mid-1970s, he created the impression within the priesthood that the Gakkai was trying to control it. Throughout the rest of the seventies, while still in the role of mediator, he continued to leak misinformation in an attempt to sabotage the Gakkai's efforts to bridge the gap and create harmony with the priests.

Yamazaki also encouraged a group of disgruntled young priests to attack the Gakkai. These priests refused to perform funeral services for Gakkai members, while at the same time asserting that unless lay believers have their funeral conducted by a Nichiren Shoshu priest, they would be damned to the hell of incessant suffering. With such threats, those priests encouraged members to quit the Gakkai and join a temple parish. Those anti-Gakkai priests later formed a group called the Shoshinkai (The Group of Correct Faith).

In January 1978, when the situation started to improve, Yamazaki wrote a document titled "Letter From a Certain Believer," which he submitted to the priesthood. In it, he alleged that the Gakkai was systematically promoting the view that its president was the true Buddha, and he instructed the priesthood how to control the Gakkai by leveraging its authority. As this document circulated within the priesthood, the situation intensified.

The Gakkai continued to try to mend its relationship with the priesthood. The situation proceeded toward a resolution when Nittatsu stated on November 7, 1978: "From now on, let us realize true harmonious unity between the priesthood and laity and protect our school" (*Seikyo Shimbun*, November 8, 1978).

Disgruntled priests, however, continued to attack the Gakkai and to encourage Gakkai members to leave the organization and join temple parishes. To end the priesthood's attack on the Gakkai and avoid further confusion, Ikeda announced his resignation as Soka Gakkai president on April 24, 1979, and Hiroshi Hojo became the fourth president of the Soka Gakkai.

On July 22 that year, Nittatsu died suddenly. Shin'no Abe, then the general administrator of Nichiren Shoshu, claimed to have received the lineage of high priest from Nittatsu on April 15, 1978. With no one contesting his claim to the high office, Abe changed his first name to Nikken and became the sixty-seventh high priest on August 6, 1979.

Yamazaki at first curried favor with Nikken so that he might continue to manipulate the priesthood and exert his influence over the Gakkai. After his attempts failed, however,

Yamazaki started questioning the legitimacy of Nikken's succession and attacking him in the media. For example, in the weekly tabloid *Shukan Bunshun* dated November 20, 1980, Yamazaki alleged that Nikken never received the lineage of high priest from his predecessor. Furthermore, Shoshinkai priests started to attack Nikken's legitimacy as high priest. In January 1981, Shoshinkai priests filed a lawsuit against Nikken, seeking to nullify his status as high priest. Starting the following year, Nikken expelled about 180 Shoshinkai priests from the priesthood.

Meanwhile, Yamazaki resigned his position as legal counsel for the Gakkai in March 1980. After his resignation, he started to attack the Gakkai overtly in the media and incited the priesthood to do the same. At that time, he was in possession of a large volume of the Gakkai's internal documents, which had been stolen by Takashi Harashima, the former Study Department chief who betrayed the Gakkai in league with Yamazaki. Yamazaki, burdened with large business debts, decided to extort money from the Gakkai by threatening to use the contents of those internal documents to fuel attacks by the priesthood and the media.

The circumstances surrounding the Gakkai at this time were complex. Around the end of 1979, Yamazaki brought several of those stolen documents to the attention of the media and the priesthood. One of them was a memorandum written in June 1974 by Hiroshi Hojo, then Soka Gakkai vice president. In 1974, the Soka Gakkai proposed to the priesthood the establishment of a Nichiren Shoshu International Center to better support its rapidly increasing overseas membership. The priesthood, however, vehemently opposed the idea, suspecting that the Gakkai was attempting to control the priesthood under the umbrella of the proposed NSIC.

Hojo, out of deep frustration, wrote a report to Ikeda, characterizing the priesthood as "a serious obstacle to kosen-rufu." He also wrote in the report: "I think that in the long run, we have no choice but to separate wisely. [The difference between the priesthood and the Soka Gakkai] is essentially similar to that of Catholicism and Protestantism." Ikeda admonished Hojo at that time for emotionalism and rejected his idea, and the Gakkai continued to support the priesthood. When this memorandum was leaked to the media and the priesthood around the end of 1979, the Gakkai found itself in an awkward position since, to explain the context of Hojo's document, the Gakkai would have to reveal the obstinate emotionalism exhibited by the priesthood regarding the NSIC. Bound by its role to support and protect the priesthood, the Gakkai was thus defenseless against the onslaught from the media and the anti-Gakkai priests.

When Yamazaki attempted to blackmail the Gakkai with a threat to leak more of the Gakkai's internal documents in April 1980, the bitter experience of the Hojo report was still fresh in the minds of the organization's senior officials. By this time, they had also become keenly aware of Yamazaki's cunning at mixing factual information with falsehoods and engineering information leaks to elicit a negative response. Because its relationship with the priesthood was still fragile, the Gakkai expected a more virulent attack from the media and the priesthood, one that would ultimately hurt the members. So Soka Gakkai senior officials made the painful decision to comply with Yamazaki's demand and pay him 300 million yen.

When Yamazaki demanded another 500 million yen, however, the Gakkai leadership decided to report everything to the authorities and press charges against Yamazaki for extortion. In January 1981, Yamazaki was arrested and, on March

26, 1985, convicted of extortion in the Tokyo District Court. He was sentenced to three years in prison, which he served from February 25, 1991, until April 27, 1993.

After his release from prison, Yamazaki allied himself with Nikken, whom he had previously attacked, as well as with anti-Gakkai politicians and journalists in his vendetta against the Gakkai.

Since well before Nikken's tenure as high priest, the Soka Gakkai maintained its dedicated support of the priesthood. With this support, the priesthood held major events, such as a weeklong service in October 1981 to celebrate the seven-hundredth anniversary of the Daishonin's passing. There was also the observance of the 650th anniversary of Nikko Shonin's passing in March 1982, and one in December of the same year to mark the 650th anniversary of third high priest Nichimoku's passing.

Furthermore, the Gakkai proposed the construction of two hundred branch temples for the priesthood. Thus, every year, the Gakkai donated many branch temples throughout the 1980s. With the Gakkai's enormous contribution, the priesthood, although it had lost many priests and branch temples through its conflict with the Shoshinkai, started to enjoy once again an unprecedented level of development and prosperity.

In his New Year's message for 1991, even as he was hatching his plan to attempt to disband the Gakkai, Nikken wrote: "Also worthy of special mention about President Ikeda's leadership is that he has greatly advanced worldwide kosen-rufu.... The many offerings to the head temple and the do-nation of local temples begun by the Soka Gakkai around the time of President Toda have been diligently carried on by President Ikeda, whose contributions have earned numerous words of praise from my predecessor" (January 1991 *Seikyo Times*, p. 3). As evident in his message, Nikken could not deny Ikeda's unprecedented contributions to the global spread of the Daishonin's Buddhism and to the priesthood's prosperity although, when he wrote this message, he had already decided to expel Ikeda and destroy the Gakkai.

Although it had witnessed numerous unmistakable signs of corruption and authoritarianism within the priesthood, especially during the late 1970s, the Gakkai continued to increase its level of support for the priesthood. In this regard, Ikeda talks about the basic stance of the Gakkai before the most recent outbreak of the temple issue at the end of 1990: "We protected the priesthood with the utmost sincerity. In recent years, as well, even while confronted with the reality of the decadence and runaway greed of priests, we have all along made known our wish that the priesthood purify itself" (from his speech on May 3, 1992, in the June 8, 1992, *World Tribune*, p. 5). Unfortunately, those years of tolerance by the Gakkai toward the priesthood were completely betrayed the moment Nikken declared his true intentions to disband the Soka Gakkai.

(See Appendix A for a chronology of events covered in this chapter.)

CHAPTER 14

Liberating the Daishonin's Buddhism

November 28, 1991, will probably be marked as one of the most memorable days in the history of Nichiren Daishonin's Buddhism. In an ultimate display of clerical authority, the Nichiren Shoshu priesthood excommunicated the SGI with its worldwide membership of more than ten million. The priesthood's sense of power rests on its ability to exclude believers from communion with the high priest, who, according to its new doctrine, is identical with the Dai-Gohonzon and Nichiren Daishonin in his spiritual properties.

Operation C

The priesthood maintains that communion with or connection to the high priest is essential for believers' salvation; the excommunicated have no hope of attaining enlightenment. From the priesthood's standpoint, therefore, excommunication is a spiritual death sentence; it is a device to evoke believers' fear and thereby demand their obedience. For this device to be effective, however, believers must be convinced that their happiness depends upon their relationship with the high priest. Since excommunication is the priesthood's last resort in its attempt to restore its superior status over believers, all it could do when this failed was to threaten excommunication again (in 1997) to those it had already excommunicated.

The 1991 excommunication was unprecedented in scale in the entire history of Buddhism and was certainly rare in any world religion. On November 7, prior to the excommunication, the priesthood sent the Gakkai a notice calling for its dissolution. On July 4, 1992, the priesthood revoked Daisaku Ikeda's status as a lay believer of Nichiren Shoshu, that is, excommunicating once again the leader of the already excommunicated lay organization. On September 29, 1997, Nichiren Shoshu held an emergency council session and revised its rules so that believers who belong to other religious groups would lose their status as believers unless they terminated their religious affiliations before the end of November (the priesthood maintained that it had excommunicated the Soka Gakkai organization but not its members). Thus, Gakkai members were once again expelled from Nichiren Shoshu on November 30, 1997. These repeated efforts to excommunicate SGI members demonstrate the failure of the priesthood's measures as well as its frustration.

Behind the priesthood's self-destructive decision to excommunicate the SGI was the high priest's insecurity over the control of the ever-growing international lay Buddhist movement as well as his animosity toward its leader. Although it cannot be denied that there was an underlying feeling of discontent and mistrust among priests toward the lay organization, something that had existed since the 1970s, what directly motivated the priesthood's hysteric behavior in punishing the SGI was sixty-seventh high priest Nikken Abe's emotionalism.

In February 1989, the priesthood proposed a large increase

in the fees paid by lay believers to visit Taiseki-ji. When Gakkai representatives asked that the priesthood reconsider the price hikes, the priesthood retracted its proposal altogether in frustration. This incident seemed to solidify Nikken's resolve to disband the Gakkai and gain control of its membership.

On July 16, 1990, Nikken and his close associates met in secrecy at Taiseki-ji's branch office in Nishikata, Tokyo. They agreed on a plan to enfeeble the Gakkai and gain control over its membership. The plan was code-named Operation C, whose meaning Nikken himself disclosed to one priest as "Operation Cut"—to "cut off Ikeda from Nichiren Shoshu and thereby from the Gakkai membership." The plan was scheduled to be implemented in August 1990. The existence of Operation C, denied by the priesthood, was proven when conference notes taken by Jitoku Kawabe, a senior priest and participant in the Nishikata meeting, were made public.

The plan describes in detail steps necessary to achieve its goal—control of the Gakkai membership. The basic steps in the plan include: 1) dismiss Ikeda as chief lay representative; 2) demand that priests comprise half of the Gakkai's Board of Directors; 3) bar Ikeda from public appearances and prohibit reports on his activities in Gakkai publications; 4) if the Gakkai does not accept these demands, excommunicate Ikeda and the lay organization; 5) run an advertisement in major newspapers for one week announcing that the Gakkai is no longer associated with Nichiren Shoshu; and 6) urge members to secede from the Gakkai and directly join their temple parish.

The following day, July 17, the priesthood held its regular communication conference with Soka Gakkai representatives. There, Gakkai leaders requested that senior officials in the priesthood admonish priests who were displaying extravagant lifestyles. This request from the Gakkai inadvertently put the priesthood in an awkward position. If it decided to launch Operation C the following month as scheduled, the action would reflect badly as an emotional reaction to the Gakkai's legitimate claim.

On July 18, Nikken called another conference at Taiseki-ji and decided to postpone the implementation of Operation C until the seven-hundredth anniversary of the head temple's founding was celebrated in October. Meanwhile, in response to the Gakkai's request, the priesthood issued a notice listing more than twenty points cautioning priests on their conduct.

On December 16, 1990, the priesthood sent a letter of inquiry to the Soka Gakkai accusing Ikeda of disrespecting the high priest and committing doctrinal errors in his speech at a Soka Gakkai Headquarters leaders meeting on November 16. The priesthood was using Ikeda's speech as a pretext to implement the once-delayed Operation C. The accusations in the priesthood's letter of inquiry, however, were based on inaccurate transcriptions of the speech and statements taken out of context, which the priesthood later admitted.

The Gakkai requested a face-to-face meeting with priesthood representatives to resolve misunderstandings through discussion rather than exchanging documents. On December 26, however, the priesthood sent the Gakkai a letter describing the Gakkai's response as "insincere." Based on the priesthood's view of itself as an absolute and unquestionable religious authority, anything short of immediate supplication to its demands would be cast as insincere or slanderous.

On December 27, 1990, the priesthood held an emergency council session and amended the school's rules to place a term limit on the offices of lay representatives. The

rule meant Ikeda's term as chief lay representative would ex-
pire immediately. The priesthood initially maintained that
the loss of Ikeda's position was merely the result of these revisions and not intended as punitive. The sequence of the
events, however, clearly indicates otherwise. This was the
first step in the temple's implementation of Operation C.

On December 25, just prior to Ikeda's dismissal, Nikken
met with active anti-Gakkai priest Kojun Takahashi and his
brother Isao Dan, an anti-Gakkai tabloid media reporter, at
the head temple. At the meeting, the high priest thanked Dan
for his long-standing critical coverage of the Gakkai and
asked him to further intensify his written attacks. Nikken
also expressed his desire to "gain 200,000 Gakkai members"
as a result of expelling Ikeda from Nichiren Shoshu. This fig-
ure, sufficient to ensure a foundation of financial contributions for all the branch temples, indicates the calculating
attitude with which Nikken executed Operation C.

On January 1, 1991, the Soka Gakkai sent a letter to the
priesthood, responding to each of the priesthood's allegations
in its original letter of inquiry. As a result, the priesthood acknowledged three transcription errors and one unsubstanti-
ated statement based on hearsay in their allegations.

On January 16, Soka Gakkai President Einosuke Akiya
sent a letter of protest to Nichiren Shoshu General Administrator Nichijun Fujimoto, pointing out the priesthood's
trumped-up charges against the Gakkai and demanding its
accountability for the incident as well as the retraction of
punitive measures taken against the Gakkai.

Meanwhile, with the priesthood's initial accusations now
proven unjustifiable, Nikken sought another pretext to pro-
ceed with Operation C in Ikeda's past statements about the
Grand Main Temple. At nationwide chief priests' meetings

held at the head temple on January 6 and 10, 1991, Nikken criticized Ikeda for his statement made on October 12, 1968, at the ceremony to mark the start of the Grand Main Temple construction. At that time, Ikeda described the Grand Main Temple as "the high sanctuary of the true teaching of the Lotus Sutra." Nikken alleged that Ikeda had attempted to define the significance of the Grand Main Temple even before the sixty-sixth high priest Nittatsu. Nikken asserted that Ikeda's statement demonstrated his arrogance in overstepping the bounds of a lay believer and that the current "problem" of the Gakkai stemmed from this arrogance.

After Nikken's speech, however, the priesthood found out that Nittatsu had indeed made statements about the significance of the Grand Main Temple as the high sanctuary prior to October 1968. Nikken's claim that Ikeda had done so first was shown to be false. In spite of the revelation, the priesthood published Nikken's speech in the February 1991 issue of *Dai-Nichiren* with a brief statement acknowledging Nittatsu's prior statements. In protest, the Gakkai sent a letter requesting a retraction and an apology. The priesthood responded in a letter dated March 9 that some of Nittatsu's statements had been inappropriate and were made under pressure from the Gakkai. On March 30, the Gakkai responded, refuting in detail the priesthood's allegations.

Despite its unsuccessful attempts to justify its claims against the Gakkai based on Ikeda's November 1990 speech and his October 1968 statement, the priesthood proceeded with its plan. It decided that from July 1991, it would abolish the Gakkai-sponsored pilgrimage to the head temple and institute a new system in which all believers must obtain a permit from the chief priest of their local branch temple to visit Taiseki-ji to worship the Dai-Gohonzon. Needless to say, the measure was devised to make Gakkai members directly dependent on their temples, where they could be encouraged to secede from the Soka Gakkai. The scheme, however, produced only small, frustrating results, which forced the priesthood to its final phase of Operation C—the excommunication of the SGI in November.

Contrary to the priesthood's expectation, however, SGI members interpreted this intended spiritual death sentence as a declaration of spiritual independence from abusive priestly authority. In an ironic reversal of the priesthood's intended purpose, the excommunication encouraged the SGI to rally under the theme of "Soka Renaissance." Nichiren Daishonin's Buddhism could now take its place as a global religion, rather than the possession of a provincial and restrictive clergy. Its humanitarian and egalitarian principles could now be directly communicated, without dogmatic constraints, to the world.

Besides Nikken's emotionalism, there are some additional underlying elements behind this conflict. These reflect behavior patterns displayed by the priesthood over the last seven centuries. First, the priesthood became so preoccupied with its own prosperity that the spread of the Daishonin's Buddhism was reduced to a means for economic gain. For example, the priesthood's aggressive promotion of funeral-related rituals, such as memorial tablets and posthumous Buddhist names, reflects the attitude that members' bereavement is merely a source of income.

The Three Powerful Enemies

Second, the priesthood continues to view lay believers as inferiors and to demand an absolute obedience similar to the feudal relationship between a lord and his vassals. This archaic attitude, which is contrary to the Daishonin's egalitarian teaching, has become a source of anxiety for the priesthood. This anxiety grew as the importance of priests to both the practice of individual believers and to propagation diminished considerably with the successful development of the lay Buddhist movement. The more the priesthood asserted its superiority and importance, the more oppressive it became toward lay believers. Trapped in this vicious cycle, the priesthood under Nikken's leadership has grown extremely authoritarian to a level never before seen in the school's history.

From the standpoint of Buddhism, the priesthood's attempt to destroy the SGI is an unavoidable obstacle to the spread of Buddhism as foretold in the Lotus Sutra and predicted and experienced by the Daishonin himself. In the "Former Affairs of the Bodhisattva Medicine King" chapter of the Lotus Sutra, Shakyamuni says to Bodhisattva Constellation King Flower: "After I have passed into extinction, in the last five hundred year period you must spread it [the Lotus Sutra] abroad widely throughout Jambudvipa and never allow it to be cut off, nor must you allow evil devils, the devil's people, heavenly beings, dragons, *yakshas* or *kumbhanda* demons to seize the advantage!" (LS23, 288).

This sutra passage describes the Buddha's mandate to spread the teachings and ideals of the Lotus Sutra throughout the world and overcome various obstacles in the process. In Buddhist history, the SGI's current state of development may be one of the few phenomena, if not the only one, that precisely correspond to the global spread of Buddhism as foretold by the sutra.

In the "Encouraging Devotion" chapter of the Lotus Sutra, the descriptions of those inevitable obstacles come vividly alive. The sutra explains that its practitioners will face three kinds of obstacles. First, they will face "many ignorant people / who will curse and speak ill" of them and attack them with "swords and staves" (LS13, 193). Second, the sutra predicts: "In that evil age there will be monks / with perverse wisdom and hearts that are fawning and crooked / who will suppose they have attained what they have not attained, / being proud and boastful in heart" (ibid.). Third, the sutra goes on: "Or there will be forest-dwelling monks / wearing clothing of patched rags and living in retirement, / who will claim they are practicing the true way, / despising and looking down on all humanity" (ibid.). Those three obstacles facing the sutra's practitioners are called the three powerful enemies of Buddhism, according to the Chinese Buddhist scholar Miaolo (711–782). The most powerful is the third kind: priests who are revered as saints and respected by the general public and who, in fear of losing fame and profit, induce the secular authorities to persecute the sutra's practitioners.

During the Daishonin's time, Ryokan, chief priest of Gokuraku-ji, a prestigious temple of the Ritsu school in Kamakura, fit the sutra's descriptions of the third powerful enemy. Ryokan was the main instigator behind the government's execution attempt on the Daishonin and his exile to Sado Island among other persecutions. Although he was considered a saintly priest by many for his promotion of public construction projects, he was amassing personal wealth behind the scenes and inciting the government to persecute the Daishonin and his followers.

In recent events, Nikken has proven to be functioning in the same way — as the third of the three powerful enemies. Using his religious authority, Nikken devised a plan to destroy the SGI and excommunicate it to gratify his personal desires. Furthermore, in league with Japan's ruling Liberal Democratic Party as well as anti-Gakkai journalists and activists, including Masatomo Yamazaki, Nikken has supported various anti-Gakkai campaigns in politics and media. For example, in October 1994, the LDP started to attack the Soka Gakkai in nationally televised Diet sessions, demanding Ikeda's testimony. The political harassment toward the Gakkai proceeded according to a plan detailed in a letter Yamazaki wrote to Nikken in late 1994.

LDP politicians incited anti-Gakkai sentiments in Japan, using the public's fear of religious organizations after the sarin gas attack in the Tokyo subway by the Aum Supreme Truth sect. The ruling party also attempted to revise the Religious Corporation Act to restrict the Gakkai's activities. Yamazaki's letter to Nikken indicates the priesthood's connection with those political attacks on the Gakkai.

Nichiren Shoshu also supported a petition drive in April 1992 demanding that the Tokyo metropolitan government, where the Gakkai is registered as a religious corporation, dissolve the Gakkai. The petition was rejected by the Tokyo governor's office, but Taiseki-ji later paid 10 million yen to petition organizer Nenko Ryu, a former Gakkai leader and longtime detractor. The priesthood also supported some weekly tabloids during those anti-Gakkai political campaigns. For example, Nichiren Shoshu collaborated with the weekly magazine *Shukan Bunshun* to publish articles critical of the Gakkai.

Nikken's dismissal of Ikeda as chief lay representative and his expulsion from Nichiren Shoshu interestingly coincide with the passage from the Lotus Sutra, which states that the sutra's practitioners "again and again . . . will be banished / to a place far removed from towers and temples" (LS13, 195).

As the Daishonin himself experienced through the persecutions induced by Ryokan, the third of the three powerful
enemies manifests itself in the form of religious authority.
Referring to Ryokan, the Daishonin states that the third
powerful enemy of Buddhism typically exhibits the characteristics of greed, jealousy, delusion, lewdness and self-in-
dulgence despite the reputation of abiding by Buddhist
precepts (GZ, 350). The third powerful enemy invariably
takes the form of religious authority in order to abuse believers and obstruct the spread of Buddhism. As the Daishonin
explains: "It is the way of the great devil to assume the form
of a venerable monk..." (WND, 81).

Nichiren Shoshu's most recent wrongdoing is twofold. First,
it excommunicated the SGI and attempted to destroy its international Buddhist movement.
To destroy a harmoniously united
group of believers is considered
to be the most serious of offenses
in Buddhism, since Buddhism
cannot benefit people without a Buddhist order dedicated to
its spread. Second, Nichiren Shoshu has distorted the Daishonin's Buddhism by presenting its priest-centered authoritarian doctrine as orthodox, thus causing profound
confusion among believers.

*Absolute Authority
of the High Priest*

To bolster the high priest's authority and thus silence
both internal and external criticism, Nichiren Shoshu has
been propounding the absolute authority of the high priest
and raising his person and administrative office to the level
of an object of religious veneration. Nichiren Shoshu asserts
that believers' faith in the high priest is as important as their
faith in the Gohonzon. In a document dated July 30, 1991,

Nichiren Shoshu senior priests stress that the high priest and the Dai-Gohonzon are "the inseparable object of veneration" and insist that believers' faith in those two must be "absolute." In a document dated September 6, 1991, the senior priests also write: "the Daishonin, who is the original Buddha, the Dai-Gohonzon of the high sanctuary, and the successive high priests are one in their internal identity and constitute an inseparable object of veneration." In the June 1991 issue of *Dai-Nichiren*, a temple believer writes: "The high priest is the modern-day Daishonin and, in his internal identity, is the object of veneration that possesses the entity of the oneness of the Person and the Law." Nichiren Shoshu Vice Study Department Chief Kosei Mizushima claims in the eleventh issue of *Fuji Gakuho*, the official publication of Taiseki-ji's seminary; "The essence or soul of the Law has been transmitted into the body of the current High Priest Nikken in the same manner as in the Daishonin's day without the slightest difference, although his appearance as an ordinary person and as a vessel of the Law may be different." Along with those doctrinal changes, Nichiren Shoshu also revised its rules and regulations so that those who criticize the high priest may be subject to punitive measures.

With those doctrinal and administrative revisions, Nichiren Shoshu has sought to establish the absolute rule of the high priest. In his sermon at a chief priests meeting on August 28, 1997, Nikken cited a letter from Nichikan, a chief priest of the temple Hosho-ji in the seventeenth century (a different person from the twenty-sixth high priest Nichikan), which was sent to Taiseki-ji's chief parishioner to solidify the fragile position of the newly appointed nineteenth high priest, Nisshun. The letter states: "The matter of Taiseki-ji [regarding the transfer of the office of high priest] is the transmission of the golden utterances [of the Buddha]. Those who receive this transmission, learned or unlearned, shall possess the living body of Shakyamuni and of Nichiren. Earnest faith in this enables the people of the Latter Day to sow the seeds of Buddhahood" (*Essential Writings of the Fuji School*, vol. 5, p. 271).

Nikken commented on this letter as follows: "Since a long time ago, I have always thought of this document as noteworthy because it explains precisely the faith of Taiseki-ji." Nikken, like Nisshun, wished to gain advantage by supporting dogma that painted the high priest as an absolute vessel of the Law and equal to the Buddha.

When faced with the three powerful enemies, the Daishonin vigorously refuted their erroneous views while expressing his powerful optimism for the spread of Buddhism. In his well-known treatise "On Establishing the Correct Teaching for the Peace

A Renaissance of the Daishonin's Buddhism

of the Land," the Daishonin sharply criticizes the teaching of the Pure Land school: "Rather than offering up ten thousand prayers for remedy, it would be better simply to outlaw this one evil" (WND, 15). When he submitted the document to the powerful retired regent Hojo Tokiyori, the Pure Land School was widespread in Japan. The Daishonin points out in the treatise that its erroneous teaching must be refuted to alleviate the confusion and suffering of the people. As shown in this passage, the Daishonin maintained an uncompromising stance toward what he saw as misleading teachings and corrupt religious authority.

Although he underwent numerous persecutions perpetrated by political and religious authority, the Daishonin's view of the three powerful enemies was positive and optimistic. He saw their appearances as proof of his identity as the votary of the Lotus Sutra as foretold by the sutra. He states: "Even if it were possible to point straight at the earth and miss it, if the flowers were to cease blooming in spring, still I am certain that these three powerful enemies exist in the land of Japan" (WND, 272).

The Daishonin's confidence in the appearance of the three powerful enemies is an expression of his confidence in his identity as the true practitioner of the Lotus Sutra as he states: "When I examine these passages, I know that, if I do not call forth these three enemies of the Lotus Sutra, then I will not be the votary of the Lotus Sutra. Only by making them appear can I be the votary" (WND, 53).

The Daishonin also viewed the appearance of the three powerful enemies as a sign of the spread of Buddhism: "Great events never have minor omens. When great evil occurs, great good follows. Since great slander already exists in our land, the great correct Law will spread without fail. What could any of you have to lament? Even if you are not the Venerable Mahakashyapa, you should all perform a dance! Even if you are not Shariputra, you should leap up and dance" (WND, 1119). No doubt such hope and optimism in the appearance of the three powerful enemies were a source of the Daishonin's resilience in facing his extreme difficulties.

The essential nature of the priesthood's recent actions is the same as that of the corrupt religious authority that persecuted the Daishonin in the thirteenth century. As Ryokan was threatened by the Daishonin's popular Buddhist movement growing in Kamakura, the priesthood views the growing influence of the laity. The priesthood's anxiety in losing its power over lay believers has brought about its recent oppression of the SGI movement. In this sense, SGI members may view the excommunication and other oppressions perpetrated by the priesthood as proof of their identity as true practitioners of the Lotus Sutra and a sign of the greater spread of the Daishonin's Buddhism in the near future.

As the Daishonin's understanding of the three powerful enemies became a source of his hope and optimism, SGI members' understanding of the recent temple issue will no doubt serve as the driving force behind the development of the Daishonin's Buddhism. The priesthood's excommunication of the SGI, in this sense, will be recorded as a pivotal moment in the history of Buddhism. It has served to announce a new era in which the Daishonin's humanistic ideals will flow unrestricted, thus marking the beginning of a real renaissance of the Daishonin's Buddhism.

CHAPTER 15

The SGI's Conferral of the Gohonzon

On September 7, 1993, about two months short of the second anniversary of its excommunication by the Nichiren Shoshu priesthood, the SGI an-

The Gohonzon: The Object of Devotion for All People

nounced its decision to issue the Gohonzon to its members worldwide. It was one of the defining moments of the SGI's lay Buddhist movement because it signaled the return of the object of devotion from the hold of clerical authority to its rightful heirs—ordinary people who practice the Daishonin's Buddhism.

Gohonzon issued by the SGI are reproduced from a Gohonzon transcribed by the twenty-sixth high priest, Nichikan, in 1720. This so-called Nichikan Gohonzon was in the possession of Joen-ji, a temple in Tochigi Prefecture, Japan, whose chief priest offered it for the Soka Gakkai's use. That chief priest, Sendo Narita, had previously seceded from Taiseki-ji in protest to the high priest's abusive policy toward the SGI. In his June 6, 1993, letter to Soka Gakkai President Einosuke Akiya, Chief Priest Narita writes: "The existing situation, in which Nikken has unjustly terminated the conferral of Gohonzon upon Soka Gakkai members, convinced me that the best and most just course—as well as the course that, I feel, would win the approval of the Daishonin—would be to enable Soka Gakkai members to receive Gohonzon based on this Gohonzon."

On August 23, 1993, the Association for the Reformation of Nichiren Shoshu and the Association of Youthful Priests Dedicated to the Reformation of Nichiren Shoshu—representing about thirty reform priests who had seceded from Taiseki-ji—issued a joint resolution supporting Narita's proposal. In it, the reform priests stated: "We declare that the Soka Gakkai is qualified in every way to confer *okatagi* Gohonzon based on the Gohonzon transcribed by High Priest Nichikan and assert that by so doing the Soka Gakkai will fulfill a sacred mission consistent with the spirit of Nichiren Daishonin." With the approval of the council and other committees, the Soka Gakkai decided to accept Chief Priest Narita's proposal.

Before this historic decision, conferral of the Gohonzon —the basis of the faith and practice of Nichiren Daishonin's Buddhism—was regarded by the priesthood as the high priest's prerogative, and lay believers had been long taught to support that view. After the excommunication in November 1991, many SGI members had been forced to practice without the Gohonzon. The priesthood had taken advantage of the situation and used its monopoly of the Gohonzon as leverage to entice Gakkai members to secede from their lay organization and join a temple parish.

Upon learning of the Gakkai's decision, the priesthood expressed its concern: "[The Soka Gakkai] will begin to independently bestow Gohonzons [*sic*], thus declaring complete independence from Nichiren Shoshu." (*NST News,*

Special Issue, p. 2). In the same publication, the priesthood also said: "The Soka Gakkai is a group that has been excommunicated by Nichiren Shoshu and has absolutely no relationship with Nichiren Shoshu" (ibid., p. 1). Those seemingly contradictory statements—declaring that the Gakkai had initiated independence, then that the priesthood's prior excommunication had severed the relationship —demonstrate the complex anxiety the priesthood felt toward its former believers. The priests wished that even after being excommunicated, lay believers would still feel dependent upon their clerical authority. They knew that their continued prosperity may depend on the return of its former believers. And this dependence upon its excommunicated laity, whom it despises, has been a source of mixed feelings.

Nikken's action to deny Gohonzon to the Soka Gakkai— the sole organization consistently dedicated to propagation this century—clearly runs counter to the Daishonin's intent in inscribing the Gohonzon, which he described as "the banner of propagation of the Lotus Sutra" (WND, 831).

Because of these circumstances—and based on its sense of responsibility as a harmoniously united order (*samgha*) of the Daishonin's Buddhism—the SGI decided to make Gohonzon available to its worldwide membership. It was a decision made solely to preserve the integrity of the Daishonin's Buddhism by replying to the sincerity of those seeking the Gohonzon and, thereby, further promoting the spread of the teaching.

Since the SGI announced its intent to confer Gohonzon, the priesthood has been denouncing this Gohonzon as counterfeit for three main reasons: 1) "It does not receive the sanction of the High Priest"; 2) "It is not bestowed by the Head Temple"; and 3) "It is arbitrarily manufactured by the Gakkai" (*Refuting the Soka Gakkai's "Counterfeit Object of*

Worship": 100 Questions and Answers, compiled by the Nichiren Shoshu Doctrinal Research Committee. Nichiren Shoshu Temple, 1996, p. 12).

The priesthood maintains that Gohonzon issued without the high priest's eye-opening ceremony is counterfeit (*NST News, Special Issue,* p. 9). According to the priesthood, however, the practical meaning of the eye-opening ceremony apparently is not that the high priest must infuse his presumed spiritual power, which he claims to have inherited from the Daishonin, into every Gohonzon issued by the head temple. Rather, the eye-opening ceremony seems to mean being sanctioned. As the priesthood states: "Up to now, the Gohonzons [*sic*] granted to believers at the branch temples have all been sanctioned by the High Priest, that is, their eyes have been opened" (*Refuting the Soka Gakkai's "Counterfeit Object of Worship": 100 Questions and Answers,* p. 37). And: "In Nichiren Shoshu from the ancient past, the High Priest's sanction was essential for everything related to the Gohonzon. The arbitrary copying of the Gohonzon and the conferral of the copies by the Gakkai today are unpardonable acts" (ibid., p. 39). All their arguments against the Nichikan Gohonzon boil down to one point: They are counterfeit because the high priest did not authorize them.

The term *arbitrary* in the temple's usage can only be interpreted to mean "in a way not according with the high priest's intention," which was essentially to punish those affiliated with the Gakkai by depriving them of the Gohonzon. However, it is the high priest's sudden denial of the Gohonzon to those seeking it that better fits the definition of an arbitrary act.

Regarding the reproduction and conferral of the Gohonzon, the priesthood maintains: "The only person who is able to transcribe the innermost enlightenment of the Dai-Gohonzon of the High Sanctuary is the High Priest who received the bestowal of the lifeblood to only a single person from the Daishonin. . . . During the seven-hundred-year history of Nichiren Shoshu, priests other than the High Priest, even if they were of eminent virtue, erudite or experts at calligraphy, have never transcribed the Gohonzon. However, there are instances where a retired High Priest transcribed the Gohonzon after being commissioned to do so by the current High Priest" (*Refuting the Soka Gakkai's "Counterfeit Object of Worship": 100 Questions and Answers,* pp. 29–30). In a nutshell, the priesthood asserts that unless Gohonzon are transcribed by the high priest and their printing sanctioned by him, they are not legitimate and constitute a grave doctrinal error.

The history of the Fuji School, however, contradicts this. There are numerous recorded instances in which priests other than the high priests transcribed Gohonzon since the earliest period of the Fuji School. According to the priesthood, those transcriptions of Gohonzon would be "unpardonable acts" since no one but the high priest can transcribe Gohonzon. Despite numerous records of such instances, however, there is no evidence of protest from anyone in the Fuji School, including the successive high priests. Its own history suggests, therefore, that the priesthood's assertions lack substance.

In February 1332, when Nikko and Nichimoku were still alive, Nissen, one of Nikko's six main disciples, transcribed a Gohonzon and conferred it to one of his parishioners (*Essential Writings of the Fuji School,* vol. 8, p. 214). There is no record of either Nikko or Nichimoku opposing Nissen's transcription.

The History of the Transcription of the Gohonzon

According to a document written in 1340 and attributed to Nichizon, one of Nikko's disciples, Nikko instructed that in the Fuji School, only one designated disciple should transcribe Gohonzon in order to keep the "lantern of the Law" lit —to keep the Gohonzon available to believers (*Complete Works of the Nichiren School*, vol. 2, p. 418). The same document records that, after the Daishonin's death, his six senior disciples started to transcribe Gohonzon, and there was no dispute among them about their right to produce transcriptions (ibid.). From those records, it may be surmised that Nikko made it a general rule that only one designated priest is to transcribe Gohonzon to maintain the order of the school.

For this reason, it was permissible for Nissen, who resided in the distant province of Sanuki, to transcribe a Gohonzon for one of his parishioners. There was no mention of any mysterious or exclusive power possessed by a high priest that would inject the Daishonin's soul into a transcribed Gohonzon. Other records further confirm this point.

During the late fourteenth century, after the deaths of the second high priest Nikko Shonin and the third high priest Nichimoku in 1333, Taiseki-ji priests other than the high priest transcribed many Gohonzon (*Essential Writings of the Fuji School*, vol. 8). For example, Nissen transcribed two Gohonzon in 1337 and one in 1338. Nichigo, one of Nikko's six new disciples at Omosu Seminary, transcribed two in 1344, two in 1345 and one in 1350. (The dates of two additional Gohonzon transcribed by Nichigo are unknown.) In 1340, Nichizon had a wooden Gohonzon made from a Gohonzon inscribed by Nichimoku. Nichimyo, one of Nikko's six disciples at Omosu Seminary, transcribed one in 1344. Nichiman, Nikko's disciple on Sado Island, transcribed one in 1352 and another in 1357. Nichidai, one of Nikko's six new disciples at Omosu

Seminary, transcribed one in 1388. While those Gohonzon were transcribed by priests other than the high priest during the tenures of the fourth high priest Nichido (1333–39), the fifth high priest Nichigyo (1339–65) and the sixth high priest Nichiji (1365–1406), none of those high priests left any record of denouncing those transcriptions as unorthodox. It is especially noteworthy that Nichigyo never accused Nichigo, his adversary in a bitter land dispute over Taiseki-ji, of transcribing Gohonzon in an unauthorized manner and thus violating the high priest's alleged prerogative.

In other words, during the early days of the Fuji School after Nikko Shonin established Taiseki-ji and appointed Nichimoku as his successor in 1290, the priesthood intended to limit the transcription of the Gohonzon to one designated person for the orderly management of the Fuji School. However, it did not consider transcription of the Gohonzon by a priest other than the high priest to be a grave doctrinal error. For this reason, Nichiu, the ninth high priest, allowed branch temple chief priests to transcribe the Gohonzon. He states in "On Formalities": "Those at branch temples who have disciples and lay patrons may transcribe the amulet [i.e., the Gohonzon]. However, they should not place their seals on it.... Those at branch temples who have disciples and lay patrons may transcribe the mandala [i.e., the Gohonzon] yet may not place their seal on it" (*Essential Writings of the Fuji School*, vol. 1, p. 71).

Those Gohonzon transcribed by chief priests at the branch temples and without the transcriber's written seal were considered temporary, conferred before believers received one transcribed by the high priest. By allowing chief priests to transcribe the Gohonzon, yet asking them not to affix their personal seals, Nichiu tried to accomplish two things: meeting the needs of believers who could not otherwise receive Gohonzon while maintaining order within the school regarding the transcription of the Gohonzon. Since Gohonzon transcribed by chief priests were considered temporary and usually without transcription date or name of a transcriber, not many of them survive today. Nonetheless, there are enough recorded instances to verify the Fuji School's practice of transcribing Gohonzon by priests other than the high priest. For example, according to Jundo Nose's *Miscellaneous Records* (Jpn Shokiroku), Nissho, a chief priest of a lodging temple on the head temple grounds, transcribed a Gohonzon for the parish of a Shinto shrine near the head temple in 1823 (vol. 7, p. 355). When Nissho transcribed this Gohonzon, the forty-ninth high priest Nisso and the retired forty-eighth high priest Nichiryo were residing at Taiseki-ji, so there was no immediate need for Nissho to transcribe a Gohonzon on behalf of the high priest. Nissho was a veteran priest at Taiseki-ji who served eight high priests, and he probably simply responded to a request from his local parish.

In 1860, Nichigen, a disciple of Nissho, also transcribed a Gohonzon for one of his parishioners (*Miscellaneous Records*, vol. 7, p. 242). The dates and the transcriber's name for this Gohonzon appear on the back probably because it was customary that only the high priest place his seal on the Gohonzon. Both Nissho and his disciple Nichigen were high-ranking priests at Taiseki-ji but did not become high priests. Nevertheless, they still transcribed Gohonzon and conferred them on their parishioners.

There are also records of Gohonzon whose transcribers are unknown. Since the high priest customarily placed his seal on Gohonzon he transcribed, it is certain that someone other than a high priest transcribed these Gohonzon. In 1760, during the tenure of the thirty-third high priest Nichigen, someone other than the high priest transcribed a Gohonzon dedicated to a Shinto deity and kept it at Honjo-ji, a branch temple of Taiseki-ji (*Miscellaneous Records* , vol. 7, p. 226).

As a side note, during the eighteenth century, many Gohonzon were transcribed for Shinto shrines near Taiseki-ji and its other branch temples, supposedly to call forth the power of Shinto deities dwelling there. Often these Gohonzon, many of which were transcribed by high priests, were requested by lay parishioners for a Shinto shrine in their home village. Such parishioners rarely understood the tenets of the Daishonin's Buddhism concerning the Gohonzon, and mixed their practice of Shintoism with other forms of Buddhism. The priests who transcribed Gohonzon for this purpose must surely have known this and that it violated the guidelines set down by Nikko Shonin, the founder of the Fuji School. One such Gohonzon, for example, bears the inscription, "Bestowed to summon forth the body of the god of the Tenman Shrine." Nevertheless, the doctrinal legitimacy of these "Shinto Shrine" Gohonzon was never questioned.

There were two Taiseki-ji priests who became chief priests of Myoren-ji, a prominent old temple near Taiseki-ji, who transcribed Gohonzon. On March 1, 1707, Nichiju became the twenty-fourth chief priest of Myoren-ji. From that time until 1727, when he left his position at Myoren-ji, he continued to transcribe Gohonzon for his parishioners and the chief priests of branch temples that belonged to Myoren-ji. (Myoren-ji and its branch temples joined Nichiren Shoshu, under the head temple Taiseki-ji, in 1950. Before that, it was regarded as one of the eight head temples of the Fuji School that maintained its own branch temples. Taiseki-ji was also one of these eight.)

According to one source, Nichiju transcribed eleven Go-honzon while he was chief priest of Myoren-ji (*Ideas of the Fuji School* [Jpn Fuji Monryu Shiko], ed. Mitsuaki Osawa; no. 4, p. 9). During this time, Nichiei (twenty-fourth), Nichiyu (twenty-fifth), Nichikan (twenty-sixth), Nichiyo (twenty-seventh) and Nissho (twenty-eighth) became high priests successively at Taiseki-ji, but none of them criticized Nichiju for transcribing Gohonzon. Neither was Nichiju ex-communicated by his teacher, Nichiei. Even after he went to Myoren-ji, Nichiju maintained friendly ties with Taiseki-ji.

In 1727, when he retired, Nichiju appointed Nichiho as chief priest of Myoren-ji. Between 1727 and 1732, Nichiho transcribed Gohonzon for his parishioners. Three of them were recorded (*Ideas of the Fuji School*, no. 4, p. 10). After he left Myoren-ji, he returned to Taiseki-ji, and in 1736, the twenty-ninth high priest, Nitto, transferred the lineage of high priest to Nichiho, who then renamed himself Nitchu. There is no record of Nitchu being criticized for having transcribed Gohonzon before he received the lineage.

Nichiju and Nitchu demonstrate the Taiseki-ji priest-hood's view that the transcription and conferral of the Go-honzon is an administrative responsibility of priests. Myoren-ji, as a head temple, had to meet the needs of its own parish and branch temples.

The nineteenth high priest, Nisshun, and the twenty-second high priest, Nisshun (same pronunciation, but writ-ten with different Chinese characters), also transcribed Gohonzon before they assumed the post of high priest. The nineteenth high priest became the chief priest of Taiseki-ji in the summer of 1641 without receiving the lineage of high priest from his predecessor, the seventeenth high priest, Nissei. Nissei had fallen out of favor with Kyodai-in, an influential lay patron, who maneuvered him out of office (see chapter 4 for more information). With strong backing from Kyodai-in, Nisshun was selected as Nissei's successor (*The Sacred Scriptures of Nichiren Shoshu* [Jpn Nichiren Shoshu Seiten], p. 763). (Editor's note: Kyodai-in was an adopted daughter of Tokugawa Ieyasu, the founder of the Edo shogunate government.)

For approximately four years, though out of office, Nissei refused to transfer the lineage. Until he finally received the lineage of high priest on October 27, 1645, Nisshun carried out various responsibilities—including the transcription and conferral of Gohonzon—as chief priest of Taiseki-ji but not as high priest of the school. There are two records of Gohonzon transcribed by Nisshun before he received the lineage of high priest. He transcribed one on January 8, 1645, and another on February 28 of the same year—approximately ten and eight months, respectively, before he received the lineage (*Miscellaneous Records*, vol. 2, p. 101; vol. 3, p. 104).

The twenty-second high priest, Nisshun, received the lineage of high priest from the twenty-first high priest, Nichinin, in 1680 (*The Chronology of Nichiren Shoshu and the Fuji School* [Jpn Nichiren Shoshu Fuji Nenpyo], p. 257). In 1676, four years earlier, however, Nisshun transcribed a Gohonzon for the parish of Shinko-ji in the Chiba area (*Miscellaneous Records*, vol. 7, p. 254). It is not certain where Nisshun was at that time, but he was not high priest of Taiseki-ji. Nisshun was the first Taiseki-ji priest who became a teacher at the Hosokusa Seminary in Chiba. Probably because of his reputation as an erudite priest, the parish of Shinko-ji near the seminary might have asked Nisshun to transcribe a Gohonzon.

In addition to the Gohonzon transcribed by persons other than the high priest, the school's history also reveals numerous records of ordinary priests reproducing the Dai-shonin's original Gohonzon as well as Gohonzon tran-scribed by some prominent high priests such as Nikko and Nichikan. In the process of reproduction, a priest would place the original beside the new reproduction and copy it as closely as possible. Or the image would be traced on thin pa-per placed atop the original. An artisan would then use the copies made in this manner to carve a wooden Gohonzon, or a wood block template, from which further reproductions would be printed.

In February 1836, for example, Nikki, the chief priest of Butsugen-ji in Sendai, copied a Gohonzon that Nikko had transcribed in 1303 and had a wooden Gohonzon made from the copy. He then removed a Gohonzon transcribed by the thirty-seventh high priest from the temple altar and en-shrined this wooden Gohonzon in its place (*Miscellaneous Records*, vol. 8, p. 215). While he described the process in writ-ing on the back of the wooden Gohonzon, Nikki did not men-tion anything about receiving sanction from the high priest at Taiseki-ji to reproduce Nikko's Gohonzon or whether the high priest conducted an eye-opening ceremony on it. (At that time, the fiftieth high priest, Nichijo, and the retired forty-eighth high priest, Nichiryo, were present at Taiseki-ji.)

According to *Miscellaneous Records*, while some wooden Gohonzon carry the high priest's signature, many others bear no such inscription or record. Furthermore, there is only one wooden Gohonzon in existence that bears a record of a high priest having performed an eye-opening ceremony upon it. This wooden Gohonzon was made after a Gohonzon tran-scribed by Nikko in 1306 (*Miscellaneous Records*, vol. 15, p. 445). Furthermore, in *Miscellaneous Records* and other docu-ments, there are many records of Gohonzon reproduced through wood block printing whose templates were produced by those other than the high priests. These include Gohonzon reproduced from the Gohonzon inscribed by the Daishonin in 1282 and kept at Kyodai-ji in Tokushima Prefecture and widely distributed throughout Japan; Gohonzon reproduced from the Gohonzon transcribed by Nikko Shonin in March 1306 and kept at Honko-ji in Shizuoka Prefecture and other temples; and Gohonzon reproduced from the Gohonzon transcribed by Nichikan in 1718 and widely distributed during the late nineteenth century and the early twentieth century.

The same 1718 Gohonzon by Nichikan was also conferred upon Gakkai members after World War II. None of these *okatagi* Gohonzon bear the high priest's signature, indicating that their templates were transcribed by someone other than a high priest. Those numerous records indicate clearly that the high priest's sanction or eye-opening ceremony was not a necessary condition for the reproduction of Gohonzon.

Some high priests of modern times have claimed that the lineage of high priest is an absolutely necessary condition for the transcription of the Gohonzon. For example, fifty-sixth high priest Nichio (1848–1922), states: "Unless one receives the bequeathal of the golden utterance to the direct successor, one can never transcribe the object of worship" (*Dispelling Illusion and Observing One's Mind* [Jpn Bennaku Kanjin Sho], p. 212, as translated in *Refuting the Soka Gakkai's "Counterfeit Object of Worship": 100 Questions and Answers*, p. 29). Nichio's claim is either an indication of his ignorance of the school's history or a blatant attempt to revise the tradition for the sake of aggrandizing the high priest's authority. In light of the recorded history of the Fuji School, the high priest's prerogative over the transcription and conferral of the Gohonzon is merely an administrative device to maintain the orderly relationship between

Taiseki-ji and its branch temples and thereby prevent internal schism. It was never meant as a doctrinal or metaphysical necessity. For this reason, there are abundant records of Gohonzon transcribed by priests without the lineage of high priest.

The current priesthood's claims against the Gohonzon issued by the SGI clearly contradict the precedents set down in the Fuji School's own history. Furthermore, the transcription from which this Gohonzon is derived was made by Nichikan, the twenty-sixth high priest recognized by both the priesthood and the Soka Gakkai as the "restorer of the Fuji School." (For more discussions regarding the reproduction of the Gohonzon and its history, please refer to "A Historical Perspective on the Transcription of the Gohonzon" and "The Recent History of the Conferral of the Gohonzon" in *Reaffirming Our Right to Happiness: On the Gohonzon Transcribed by High Priest Nichikan*, published by the SGI-USA in 1996.)

When the priesthood excommunicated it in 1991, the SGI was liberated from the priesthood's authoritarianism in several important areas. The SGI's decision to issue Gohonzon to its worldwide membership in 1993 freed the lay Buddhist movement from myths promulgated by the priesthood that had long shrouded the significance of the Gohonzon.

The True Meaning of the Gohonzon

Before this epochal decision, the priesthood deliberately led lay believers to think that they must leave matters concerning the Gohonzon—especially its transcription, printing and conferral—to the priesthood because they involve a level of mysticism beyond the grasp of ordinary practitioners. The priesthood's attitude toward the Gohonzon also promoted the tendency to view the Gohonzon as an external entity endowed with mysterious powers that control the lives of believers.

The SGI's conferral of Gohonzon, however, has helped to clarify correct faith in the Gohonzon. It is no longer a magical object, the understanding of which is veiled by an alleged mysterious and exclusive heritage of an elite individual —the high priest. Meanwhile, the truly "mystic" quality of the Gohonzon has been made clear: that is, its power to call forth, in response to the believer's powers of faith and practice, the "Gohonzon"—the enlightened life-state of Buddhahood equal to that of the Daishonin—from within each believer's life. As the Daishonin states: "Never seek this Gohonzon outside yourself. . . . This Gohonzon also is found only in the two characters for faith" (WND, 832). Put another way, from the viewpoint of SGI members, the Gohonzon has ceased to be an object of spiritual dependency and has become the genuine object of their religious devotion and practice as intended by the Daishonin—a mirror to reflect their own inner enlightenment.

* The section on the history of the transcription of the Gohonzon in this installment is partly based on Mikio Matsuoka's pamphlet *A Historical Perspective on the Transcription of the Gohonzon in the Taiseki-ji School* (Jpn Taiseki-ji monryu no honzon shoshaken ni kansuru shiteki kosatsu), published by the Institute of Oriental Philosophy in 1997.

CHAPTER 16

The Destruction of the Grand Main Temple

In his sermon at Taiseki-ji on April 5, 1998, High Priest Nikken revealed his plan to transfer the Dai-Gohonzon from the Grand Main Temple to the newly renovated Hoan-den on the head temple grounds.

After attributing Japan's recent earthquake, volcanic eruption and tsunami to "the great slander of Ikeda's Soka Gakkai," Nikken stated that the SGI has become "the organization with which the great Law of Nichiren Shoshu must not be allowed to have any relationship." He then referred to the Grand Main Temple as "the largest thing to which they [SGI members] were related in the past." The high priest justified his decision by saying, "In order to completely refute the great slander of Ikeda and others, it is now most appropriate to transfer the Dai-Gohonzon out of the Grand Main Temple as quickly as possible."

Toward the end of his sermon, Nikken also stated that he would take "measures appropriate to the current circumstances" about the Grand Main Temple, which he described as "useless ruins of gigantic stature." He also hinted at his plan to build a new hall of worship, which he called "Ho'an-do." The demolition of the Grand Main Temple soon began, despite strong voices of protest from SGI members as well as from architectural and academic communities around the world. By the end of 1998, the once-majestic structure was leveled.

The Grand Main Temple was built in 1972 to house the Dai-Gohonzon. Its construction was supported by approximately 8 million Soka Gakkai members in Japan and overseas who donated more than ¥35.5 billion (approximately $100 million at the exchange rate of the time). At the time of the temple's completion, Nittatsu Hosoi, the sixty-sixth high priest, declared the Grand Main Temple to be "a great edifice that shall be the high sanctuary of the temple of the true teaching at the time of kosen-rufu."

On October 11, 1972, when the Dai-Gohonzon was transferred from the Hoan-den to the Grand Main Temple, Nittatsu further clarified the significance of the new building. He said: "I have decided that from now on and for all eternity we will worship this Gohonzon of the high sanctuary at this Grand Main Temple and pray for the believers' attainment of Buddhahood in their present forms as well as for the fulfillment of their great desires of the present and future existences, thereby designating [the Grand Main Temple] to be the great edifice in which to pray for world peace."

Nichiren Shoshu's doctrines concerning the lineage and infallibility of the high priest state that the pronouncements of a high priest must be upheld and honored as sacred. Yet Nikken's transfer of the Dai-Gohonzon out of the Grand Main Temple clearly contradicts the previous high priest's intentions.

This and the building's subsequent demolition also contradict Nikken's past statements in support of his predecessor. For example, on March 26, 1972, Nikken, who was then Nichiren Shoshu Study Department chief, stated, "Naturally, at the time of kosen-rufu, the Grand Main Temple of Taiseki-ji will become the high sanctuary mandated in 'On the Three Great Secret Laws' and the 'Minobu Transfer Document.'"

Nikken abruptly reversed his position immediately after implementing Operation C. He announced his sudden change of stance in sermons on January 6 and 10, 1991, shortly after the priesthood took the first of its punitive measures against the SGI by dismissing Daisaku Ikeda as chief representative of all Nichiren Shoshu lay organizations. He indicated that the significance of the building as the high sanctuary at the time of kosen-rufu was not a certainty. In retrospect, it is clear that through this reversal, Nikken was laying the groundwork for the building's demolition.

In these January 1991 sermons, Nikken claimed that Ikeda arrogantly overstepped his bounds as a lay believer by referring to the Grand Main Temple as the high sanctuary at its groundbreaking ceremony on October 12, 1968. The high priest claimed that no one in Nichiren Shoshu—not even High Priest Nittatsu—had ever referred to the Grand Main Temple as the high sanctuary mentioned in the Daishonin's "On the Three Great Secret Laws." Nikken asserted that Ikeda dared to define the significance of the Grand Main Temple without the high priest's instruction. He attributed the conflict between the priesthood and the SGI to this instance of Ikeda's alleged arrogance and subsequent failure to issue an apology.

But when the text of Nikken's two sermons appeared in the February 1991 issue of the *Dai-Nichiren*, the priesthood's study journal, there were some significant revisions. Added to the texts of his sermons was the statement: "I wish to amend my remarks because I discovered some statements made by High Priest Nittatsu prior to 1968 regarding the significance of the Grand Main Temple which make reference to 'On the Three

Great Secret Laws' and the 'Minobu Transfer Document.'"
This correction effectively nullified Nikken's accusations.

Although the SGI, in an open letter to the priesthood,
pointed to the lack of grounds for his accusations, Nikken
never responded to the SGI or amended his position regarding the significance of the Grand Main Temple. It is now
clear that as early as the beginning of 1991, Nikken was attempting to lay a doctrinal basis for the demolition of the
Grand Main Temple. (For more information about Nikken's
1991 sermons and the SGI's letter of inquiry, see *Issues Between the Nichiren Shoshu Priesthood and the Soka Gakkai*,
vol. 4, published by the Soka Gakkai International in 1992.)

Nikken's removal of the Dai-Gohonzon from the Grand
Main Temple and his subsequent demolition of the building
have important implications. First, Nikken's sudden decision reflects his autocratic rule within Nichiren Shoshu. Although some reformist priests had warned of the possibility
of the Dai-Gohonzon's removal from the Grand Main Temple as early as 1997, the high priest's announcement and subsequent transfer of the Dai-Gohonzon came as a surprise to
most of the more than seven hundred chief priests of
Nichiren Shoshu temples, including those assigned to lodging temples on the head temple grounds.

The notice outlining the high priest's decision was transmitted by facsimile to branch temples on the night of April 5,
1998. It states that the high priest, "reflecting upon the recent
great slander committed by Daisaku Ikeda's Soka Gakkai,
gave the profound guidance that it would be in accord with
the true intent of the founder Nichiren Daishonin to transfer
the Dai-Gohonzon of the high sanctuary of True Buddhism
back to the Hoan-den from the Grand Main Temple, which
was built at the request of Daisaku Ikeda."

The removal of the Dai-Gohonzon was planned and implemented by Nikken's close associates and Taiseki-ji's Department of Internal Affairs. Compared to the openness and grandeur of the transfer ceremony held in 1972 upon completion of the Grand Main Temple, the 1998 transfer was conducted by a small group of priests at dusk. At a service held the next day, the high priest explained that the plan had been carried out abruptly due to "circumstances that allowed no prior discussion." He apologetically added that the details of the decision would be published in the April 10 issue of *The Daibyakuho*, the organ of Nichiren Shoshu's lay organization. One can easily speculate that the suddenness of the move, and its communication only after the fact, was intended to forestall any opposition from within the ranks of the priesthood or the Hokkeko laity. Once the Dai-Gohonzon was moved, opposing the decision was an exercise in futility. Such tactics underscore the autocratic nature of Nikken's leadership.

The second important implication of Nikken's removal of the Dai-Gohonzon and his destruction of the Grand Main Temple is the contradiction of his predecessor's instruction. According to the current priesthood, all successive high priests have received a mysterious transmission from the Daishonin, so each high priest's instructions must be revered and followed as if they were the instructions of the Daishonin himself. Nikken's contradiction of his predecessor's teaching regarding the Grand Main Temple is of note since it indicates the priesthood's current dogma regarding the high priest's infallibility is arbitrary. It is cited only where it is convenient in silencing criticism toward the current high priest.

Nikken claims to have received the lineage of the high priest position from the sixty-sixth high priest Nittatsu. Yet, by destroying the Grand Main Temple, Nikken clearly went against his predecessor's instructions. On April 28, 1972, Nittatsu issued an official statement titled "Admonition" to clarify the significance of the Grand Main Temple. It reads: "The Grand Main Temple is the actual high sanctuary of this time. . . . In other words, the Grand Main Temple is a great edifice that shall be the high sanctuary of the temple of the true teaching at the time of kosen-rufu." In his sermon on April 5, 1998, Nikken claimed that the Soka Gakkai "applied pressure" on the priesthood to define the Grand Main Temple as the high sanctuary at the time of its construction. Yet, Nittatsu himself, in the face of similar allegations by anti-Gakkai factions within Nichiren Shoshu, clearly stated: "My true intent does not lie outside my admonitions and sermons." The demolition of the Grand Main Temple, in this sense, was the demolition of the priesthood's own doctrine concerning the authority of the high priest.

Furthermore, Nikken's decision also constituted a gross deception of the laity. Previously, he had made many statements in support of Nittatsu's view on the Grand Main Temple. For example, in March 1972, as Nichiren Shoshu Study Department chief, Nikken stated: "Naturally, at the time of kosen-rufu, the Grand Main Temple of Taiseki-ji will become the high sanctuary mandated in 'On the Three Great Secret Laws' and the 'Minobu Transfer Document.'" In the postscript of *On the High Sanctuary* published in December 1974, Nikken states: "At that time [of kosen-rufu], the present Grand Main Temple will be the main hall of the temple of the true teaching. This is clear from the 'Admonition' issued on April 28, 1972." Furthermore, in October 1982, commemorating the tenth anniversary of the completion of the Grand Main Temple, Nikken states as high priest: "The Grand Main Temple is a fundamental place to observe Buddhist teachings

and precepts where the people of the world repent and erad-
icate their sins. It is an edifice that is most suited for the conditions of the present time of world kosen-rufu both in its
name and substance."

If Nikken was pressured, as he claims, into adopting the
position of Nittatsu and the Soka Gakkai, then, as Study Department chief of the priesthood, he was knowingly misleading eight million believers in supporting their donation of
millions of dollars to a construction project whose fundamental significance he did not believe in.

In his April 1998 sermon, Nikken explained that he decided to remove the Dai-Gohonzon "in order to completely
refute the grave slanders of Ikeda and others." Thus
Nichiren Shoshu under Nikken has set forth a doctrinal basis for the destruction of the Grand Main Temple. Because
it was built by the Soka Gakkai and Ikeda, whom the priesthood has deemed to be slanderers, it should be torn down.
Nikken seems somehow to be implying that the tearing
down of temples donated to his school by those he now
deems slanderers is an act of refuting slander. Yet many temples in Nichiren Shoshu were once temples of other Bud-
dhists sects. They were built and donated by people with
erroneous views of Buddhism. Yet they have never been torn
down. In fact, neither Nichiren Daishonin, nor any high
priest of the Fuji School before Nikken had ever demolished
a building on the grounds that it had been built or donated
by slanderers. There is absolutely no doctrinal or historical
precedent for such an action.

In addition, if the Grand Main Temple must be destroyed
simply because it was built at the request of the SGI president
and by the donations of Soka Gakkai members, logic and
faithfulness to principle would demand that Nichiren Shoshu

also vacate, if not demolish, all other buildings and properties donated by the Gakkai—approximately 80 percent of Taiseki-ji's current real estate holdings as well as a number of large structures and numerous lodging temples on the head temple grounds. Since Ikeda was inaugurated as the third president in 1960, the Soka Gakkai built and donated 320 temples to the priesthood. In addition, the Gakkai has funded the complete or partial renovation of many existing temples.

While Nikken claims that the Grand Main Temple had to be destroyed because the SGI has become "the organization with which the great Law of Nichiren Shoshu must not be allowed to have any relationship," he clearly fails to apply the same logic or principle to the priesthood's other buildings and properties donated by the Soka Gakkai. This lack of consistency and self-contradiction can be best understood when we view Nikken's justification of the destruction as the elimination of slander as a pretext. The purpose of this pretext was to rationalize an act that was actually arbitrary and motivated by emotional resentment.

The demolition of the Grand Main Temple, in an ironic reversal of Nikken's intent to "refute the slander of Ikeda and others," actually awakened many SGI members to the essential meaning of the high sanctuary in the Daishonin's Buddhism.

The Meaning of the High Sanctuary

The high sanctuary is one of the Three Great Secret Laws; that is, one of three core elements of Nichiren Daishonin's Buddhism. These three are the object of devotion of true Buddhism (i.e., the Gohonzon), the invocation of true Buddhism (Nam-myoho-renge-kyo) and the high sanctuary of true Buddhism. These are called "secret" because they had been never revealed before the Daishonin. Needless to say, the Daishonin's intent was to make those "secrets" to happiness and peace known to all people. While it is easily understandable that the Gohonzon and Nam-myoho-renge-kyo are viewed as essential to the Daishonin's Buddhism, the importance of the high sanctuary, which is really a building, needs some explanation.

The term *high sanctuary* is an interpretation of a Chinese term that, more literally, means "precept platform" or "ordination platform." This originally meant a place of religious practice where people accept various ascetic precepts—rules of practice and discipline—which they agree to uphold to achieve their salvation. In the Daishonin's Buddhism, however, there is no need to keep such austere precepts, because practicing with sincere faith in the Gohonzon alone is equivalent to accepting all the Buddhist precepts. All we need to attain enlightenment is our faith and practice.

For this reason, wherever people practice the Daishonin's Buddhism with faith in the Gohonzon is generally regarded as the high sanctuary of true Buddhism. But the Daishonin also talks of the high sanctuary with more specificity: "When the sovereign of the nation establishes this Law, the high sanctuary of the temple of the true teaching shall be built at Mount Fuji" (*Gosho Zenshu*, p. 1600). So while the high sanctuary is generally where people practice Buddhism with faith, he also envisioned a very specific place where those committed to propagating the Mystic Law would gather.

It must be noted, however, that the Daishonin does not simply ask his future disciples to build a hall of worship. He makes it clear that the high sanctuary be built "when the sovereign of the nation establishes this Law." In other words, the high sanctuary must be built only as a result of the wide spread of his teaching. "The sovereign of the nation" in our present democratic age essentially means the people. Put simply, the substance of the high sanctuary cannot be limited to a physical structure; it essentially lies in the propagation of the Daishonin's Buddhism.

The true meaning of the high sanctuary is to be found in our faith as well as in our efforts to spread the Daishonin's Buddhism. In this sense, it may be said that the three most important elements in the Daishonin's Buddhism (i.e., the Three Great Secret Laws) are the Gohonzon, Nam-myoho-renge-kyo and the wide spread of Buddhism through individual believers' sincere faith. The Daishonin established the first two himself, and he entrusted his future disciples with the last, which gives meaning to the first two.

Nikken's demolition of the Grand Main Temple, in a sense, helped SGI members remind themselves of the real significance of the high sanctuary and reaffirm their commitment to propagate the Daishonin's Buddhism. As long as SGI members continue to spread the Daishonin's Buddhism, the Three Great Secret Laws remain intact, even though the Grand Main Temple no longer stands. However, if efforts for propagation cease, then the Daishonin's Buddhism becomes incomplete, no matter how magnificent an edifice may be built.

Thus, Nikken's destruction of the Grand Main Temple, has encouraged SGI members to internalize the meaning of the high sanctuary. And to fully realize the inner implications and significance of any event or phenomena is the proper spirit of Buddhism.

Epilogue

Learning From the Past

This book traces the history of the Fuji School, a denomination of Nichiren Buddhism founded by Nikko Shonin at Taiseki-ji toward the end of the thirteenth century. A review of the school's history helps to shed light on the current condition of Nichiren Shoshu and the current priesthood's assertions—especially, its dogma concerning the high priest's infallibility.

Like any other religious movement, there are light and dark sides in the Fuji School's seven-century history. The school has seen some exemplary priests who earnestly strove to extol, protect and spread Nichiren Daishonin's Buddhism. Nikko Shonin, the school's founder, upheld his mentor's intent against the corruption and distortions perpetrated by the five senior priests whom the Daishonin designated to help Nikko Shonin lead the Buddhist order after his death. By taking an uncompromising stance toward the five senior priests, Nikko Shonin proved the validity of the transmission of Buddhism that he had received from the Daishonin. Nikko's legitimacy, in other words, rested entirely upon his faith and understanding, which he demonstrated in his practice and efforts of propagation not only when the Daishonin was alive, but also after his death. The transmission of Buddhism from the Daishonin to Nikko Shonin, in this sense, serves as a prototype showing present practitioners how they may inherit the Daishonin's Buddhism and practice it.

Another exemplary priest in the history of the Fuji School is Nichikan, the twenty-sixth high priest. Like Nikko Shonin, Nichikan proved himself as the Daishonin's true disciple by challenging the erroneous teachings that his predecessors had brought into the school. Just as Nikko Shonin strictly pointed out the errors of the five senior priests in worshipping Shakyamuni's statue as an object of devotion, Nichikan refuted the same errors committed by his predecessors and reestablished the Gohonzon as the correct and only object of devotion in the Daishonin's Buddhism. Without Nikko and Nichikan, it would be hard to imagine that anyone today could have a correct understanding or practice of the Daishonin's Buddhism. Their legacies serve as a guide to our practice.

Whereas some high priests at Taiseki-ji, such as Nikko and Nichikan, exemplified the Daishonin's Buddhism through their actions and intent, their number is unfortunately few. As we have learned from the Fuji School's recorded history, many high priests distorted the Daishonin's Buddhism while asserting the authority they had inherited. Their actions betrayed the Daishonin's intent. For example, in the fourteenth century, Taiseki-ji was divided into two camps that for more than seventy years fought bitterly over claims to the head temple property. During the seventeenth century, several high priests accepted and promoted erroneous traditions from other Nichiren schools, such as the worship of Shakyamuni's statue. As recently as the twentieth century, high-ranking priests contended for the seat of high priest through a fraudulent election process.

As this series has highlighted using the school's own records, such examples of corruption and error among leading priests abound in the history of the Fuji School. But what value is there in reviewing these errors of the past?

First, through understanding the history of the Daishonin's Buddhism, we can view the present condition of the Nichiren Shoshu priesthood in context. The current problems within the priesthood that have resulted in its attacks on the SGI did not begin suddenly in 1990 when Nikken hatched his plan to do away with the lay organization. Nikken was able to do what he did because conditions that were conducive to his plan already existed within the priesthood. The majority of priests held that they were inherently superior to lay believers, with many feeling threatened by and jealous toward the large and growing lay Buddhist movement. Viewing the high priest as an absolute authority was a familiar concept. For many priests, direct control over believers took priority over the spread of the Daishonin's Buddhism. Temple services and rituals, such as conducting funerals and the sale of memorial tablets, had long been viewed primarily as sources of income.

These conditions made the idea of protecting their authority, and the enterprise that stemmed from that authority, a cause that most priests could support. The perceived threat to that authority in the minds of many priests was a lay organization that was enthusiastically supported and appreciated by the believers. Put another way, the unprecedented development of the SGI stemming from the pure faith and effort of the laity juxtaposed with the priesthood's seven-century-old pattern of authoritarianism and corruption made the current situation a historical certainty. If it weren't Nikken, someone else within the priesthood would have taken advantage of tensions that arose between the two groups. By understanding more about the school's history, we can gain insight into the causes of the current problems, causes that are rooted centuries in the past. With knowledge of the past, we can gain a broader perspective on the present —the reason why things are the way they are and insight as to what should be done.

A second benefit of learning about the Fuji School's past is our realization that at the core of the priesthood's corruption lie human weaknesses we are all familiar with: arrogance, jealousy and greed. Cloistered behind the veil of clerical authority for centuries, these delusions became deeply rooted in the collective psyche of the priesthood. This is not a unique situation in the history of religion. Any religious movement can become corrupt and degenerate when its leaders cease to be diligent in combating those human frailties within themselves. To spread the Daishonin's Buddhism and ensure its transmission to future generations, therefore, we must not repeat the errors of the priesthood. We are not immune to the potential for rigid authoritarianism and dogmatism simply because ours is a lay movement. With an understanding of the past, we can better guide ourselves and our Buddhist movement into the future.

Finally, by tracking the tortuous path of the Fuji School over the past seven centuries, we can better grasp the significance of the SGI and its mission in a broad historical and global context. Following the deaths of Nikko Shonin and Nichimoku in 1333, the true vigor and spirit of the Daishonin's Buddhism became dormant for centuries, with a few sporadic periods of revival, such as that of Nichikan's tenure in the early eighteenth century. The Daishonin's teaching gave rise to many different schools of so-called Nichiren

Buddhism. But their tenets and practices stray significantly from the Daishonin's original intent. As we have examined in this series, the same is true of the Fuji School. When Makiguchi and Toda founded the Soka Gakkai in 1930, the Daishonin's Buddhism had been existing in form but not in substance; that is, its practitioners had not been dedicated to its spread for the happiness of all people. And until Soka Gakkai members brought the Daishonin's Buddhism to the rest of the world, the Daishonin's promise for the global spread of his teaching had rung hollow. It was the Soka Gakkai, in fact, that revived the Daishonin's Buddhism after almost seven centuries of dormancy. Through the efforts of SGI members, the Daishonin's teaching has taken on concrete meaning in the lives of more than ten million people throughout the world.

It is no coincidence that this unprecedented spread of the Daishonin's Buddhism by lay believers rattled the priesthood's authoritarianism at its core. Our understanding of what has transpired in the years since the time of Nichiren Daishonin, Nikko and Nichimoku, makes us aware that we are practicing the Daishonin's Buddhism at a most important juncture in its history. That is, our understanding and practice of the Daishonin's teaching will determine its further development or decline from this point on.

We stand at the threshold of an entirely new stage of development. In light of this realization, the so-called temple issue no longer pertains merely to the priesthood's misconduct. It is really about the unprecedented renewal of Nichiren Buddhism—the true renewal of Buddhism and humanism—into the new millennium. As such the term "temple issue" is a bit limiting.

We can make sense of history when we understand how it

affects us today, when we understand that the past is part of our present lives. It may be difficult to say what effect the event that took place at Taiseki-ji in 1482, for example, has on our practice today. In this year, the ninth high priest, Nichiu, transferred the office of high priest to a thirteen-year-old boy. Following the appointment, Nikkyo, one of the young high priest's strong supporters, began a series of writings extolling the lineage and authority of the high priest. Nikkyo may be considered one of the key authors of the dogma of the high priest's absolute authority.

Needless to say, understanding the history of the Fuji School does not provide us with everything we need to grasp the circumstances surrounding the issues between the Nichiren Shoshu priesthood and the Soka Gakkai. More than ever, we must return to a thorough study of the basics of the Daishonin's Buddhism and deepen our understanding of what it means to practice his teaching today. Knowing our past, however, helps us realize the importance of taking such action.

Appendix A

Timeline for the Temple Issue in the 1970s

October 12: The dedication ceremony for the Grand Main Temple is held. After the completion of the Grand Main Temple, the Soka Gakkai embarks on "the second chapter of kosen-rufu" in which it engages in the construction of community centers, a broad-based approach to the Daishonin's Buddhism as a life philosophy, and the development of the Gakkai as a religious corporation. The priesthood misinterprets the Gakkai's "second chapter" as preparation for its independence. Concerned about possibly fewer future assignments to branch temples as chief priests, many young student priests in particular react negatively to the Gakkai's emphasis on the construction of community centers.

1972

June: The priesthood's mismanagement of its property is revealed in a land dispute. The deputy chairperson of the Fujinomiya City council and others file a complaint against Nittatsu and Mr. Ikeda over Taiseki-ji's illegal use of a city highway for the construction of the Grand Main Temple. This legal problem raises a concern for the priesthood's management procedures.

1973

May–July: The priesthood misconstrues the Gakkai's proposal to establish a Nichiren Shoshu International Center (NSIC) as a step toward control over the priesthood. Later, Mr. Ikeda meets with Nittatsu twice to explain the purpose of the NSIC, which is to support overseas members. Nittatsu's misunderstanding is gradually resolved, and he agrees to the establishment of the NSIC and attends the first International Buddhist League (later renamed SGI) World Peace Conference held in Guam on Jan. 26, 1975.

1974

August: The Gakkai offers to help the priesthood conduct an internal audit on its accounting and property management procedures. The priesthood administration reacts strongly, however, alleging that the Gakkai is attempting to intervene in the priesthood's finances and internal affairs. Mr. Ikeda's explanations resolve Nittatsu's misunderstanding.

April: Masatomo Yamazaki, then chief legal counsel for the Soka Gakkai, receives approval from the head temple administration to sell a large tract of its land to a paper company owned by Yamazaki. The property is then sold and bought again to inflate its price before the Gakkai purchases it for a memorial park. Yamazaki earns a large personal profit from these real estate transactions.

1975

Members of the Myokankai, a group of priests who were ordained under Nittatsu, start to criticize the Gakkai. Many priests who are active in the Myokankai will later form the Shoshinkai. With the backing of Nittatsu as their teacher, the Myokankai priests start to enjoy dominance over other factions within the priesthood.

1976

January–March: Soka Gakkai youth division members visit active Myokankai members, refute their criticism of the Gakkai and obtain statements of contrition for their mistreatment of its members.

1977

January 15: Mr. Ikeda gives a speech titled "A Historical View of Buddhism" at the ninth general meeting of the Study Department. In the speech, he comments: "Anyone who sincerely devotes himself to the dissemination of Buddhist teachings and works for the salvation of the common people is qualified to receive offerings or support from the Buddhist community. . . . In general we of the Soka Gakkai who embrace the Gohonzon and chant daimoku are 'great teachers of the Law.' In other words, we are the true *shukke* or clergy of today. Lay believers and clergy members are in fact absolutely equal in rank" (April 1977 *Seikyo Times*, pp. 9–11). "We have seen that the temples were originally places where those engaged in the practice of Buddhism could gather together, study the Buddhist teachings, and prepare themselves for the task of disseminating those teachings abroad. . . . In this sense, the community and training centers of the Soka Gakkai are worthy of being called the 'temple of the present'" (ibid., p. 11). Many priests, outraged by those remarks, start to rebut them in the priesthood's publications.

Summer: Active anti-Gakkai priests of the Myokankai provide the media with internal information to further attack the Gakkai. Weekly tabloids, such as *Shukan Shincho* and *Shukan Bunshun*, start to publish articles slandering the Gakkai. Yamazaki orchestrates these media attacks behind the scene. Using those tabloids, priests intensify their attack on the Gakkai in their sermons, encouraging Gakkai members to sever their affiliation with the Gakkai and join a temple parish.

September 22: Nittatsu issues a notice to chief priests of branch temples, expressing his "regret" over the publicized schism between the priesthood and the Gakkai. But the priests' organized movement to entice Gakkai members to leave and join a temple parish continues to increase its momentum. The media attacks on the Gakkai continue as well.

December 4: Mr. Ikeda attends a completion ceremony of Jozen-ji's main sanctuary in Miyazaki Prefecture. In his speech, he expresses his desire for harmonious unity between the priesthood and laity and pledges to support and protect the priesthood while asking for tolerance on the priesthood's part. With Mr. Ikeda's initiative and efforts, the situation starts to improve.

January 2: Nittatsu issues an "Admonition" to urge both the priesthood and laity to advance in harmony. In the same month, however, active anti-Gakkai priests continue to denounce the Soka Gakkai in their monthly sermons.

1978

January 18: Yamazaki sends his document titled "Letter From a Certain Believer" to Nittatsu. In it, Yamazaki alleges that the Gakkai is promoting the concept that its president is the true Buddha and attempting to control the priesthood. The document also offers a step-by-step plan to control the Gakkai with the threat of excommunication, and urges the priesthood to bring the Gakkai into submission within several years. The document is read at a meeting of young priests at the head temple the following day. The document undermines the possibility of reconciliation and incites priests to intensify their attacks on the Gakkai and to urge its members to join a temple parish.

February 9: The chairperson of the Nichiren Shoshu

council, the chiefs of greater parishes and active anti-Gakkai priests meet at the head temple to discuss the possibility of excommunicating the Soka Gakkai. They decide to distribute a questionnaire among the priesthood concerning the subject.

February 12 & 14: Mr. Ikeda meets Nittatsu at the head temple. As a result of their talk, the Gakkai's excommunication is averted, and the topic of the proposed questionnaire is changed to how the priesthood can cooperate with the Gakkai. Active anti-Gakkai priests express opposition to this accord.

March 14: At a nationwide meeting of priests at the head temple, Nittatsu instructs those present to work toward a harmonious relationship with the Gakkai.

March 28: The Nichiren Shoshu council passes a proposed agreement with the Gakkai, and the relationship between the priesthood and laity appears to be restored.

End of March: Yamazaki meets with Nittatsu and gives him a document titled "Future Strategy." In the document, Yamazaki recommends that the priesthood continue to apply pressure on the Gakkai with an expressed threat to excommunicate or disband the lay organization. He also instructs the priesthood to demand that the Gakkai acknowledge what the priesthood asserts are doctrinal deviations. The priesthood's response to the Gakkai henceforward proceeds according to Yamazaki's plan. Yamazaki hints to Soka Gakkai officials that if they appoint him as a mediator, harmony with the temple will be restored. Meanwhile he continues to leak manipulated internal information of the Gakkai to the media. Encouraged by the intense media attack on the Gakkai, many priests begin to vehemently criticize it in their monthly sermons.

May 8: The Gakkai appoints Yamazaki as a mediator with the priesthood.

June 30: As demanded by the priesthood, the Gakkai publishes an acknowledgement of its so-called doctrinal deviations in the *Seikyo Shimbun*. The article, titled "Basic Questions of Study," cautions Gakkai members on the usage of various Buddhist terms and expressions. The issues raised in this article strongly suggest the priesthood's frustration and insecurity toward a growing lay Buddhist movement. Taking advantage of this article, many priests, in their sermons and other temple activities, continue to threaten and entice Gakkai members to leave the organization and join a temple parish.

August 26: The first Nichiren Shoshu temple members' kick-off meeting is held at Taiseki-ji with approximately six thousand temple members attending. At the meeting, the participants decide to promote a petition seeking Mr. Ikeda's dismissal from the position of chief lay representative, a campaign to demand reimbursement of the financial contributions they had made while Gakkai members, as well as a movement to encourage Gakkai members to quit the Gakkai and directly join a temple parish.

September: Anti-Gakkai priests start to accuse the Gakkai of committing slander by having eight wooden Gohonzon made. Although these wooden Gohonzon are produced with Nittatsu's approval, many priests use the event as a pretext to further attack the Gakkai. To appease these priests, the Gakkai returns seven of the wooden Gohonzon to the head temple. With Nittatsu's approval, one wooden Gohonzon, produced from a Gohonzon transcribed for the Soka Gakkai Headquarters in 1951 by Nissho, the sixty-fourth high priest, remains enshrined at the Soka Gakkai Headquarters.

September 25: Yamazaki delivers two documents to Nittatsu. One is titled "On the Current Circumstances," and another "Regarding the Overseas Membership." In the first, Yamazaki instructs the priesthood to continue its campaign to disparage the Gakkai and bring its members to temple parishes. In the same document, he recommends that the priesthood administration exclude the Hayase and Abe family factions from key positions within the priesthood. In "Regarding the Overseas Membership," Yamazaki urges the priesthood administration to establish an overseas bureau to promote its campaign to increase temple parish members outside Japan as well.

November 7: A Soka Gakkai leaders meeting is held at Taiseki-ji. Hiroshi Hojo, then general director, states: "In this vein, we, the Soka Gakkai, frankly admit the next two points: 1) The fundamental principles that the Soka Gakkai must follow through as the lay organization of Nichiren Shoshu were somehow disregarded during the last several years in its orientation, in its direction of advance and in its application of Nichiren Daishonin's teachings. 2) The attitude the Soka Gakkai took toward Nichiren Shoshu last year was out of bounds. We, executives of the Soka Gakkai, deeply apologize for these two points" (February 5, 1979, *World Tribune*). At the same meeting, Takehisa Tsuji, then vice president, states: "As far as the wooden Gohonzons that the Soka Gakkai carelessly allowed to be inscribed, we have already dedicated them all to the Treasure House of the head temple based on the guidance we received from the high priest" (ibid.). The manuscripts of the Gakkai officials' speeches for this meeting have been checked in advance by the priesthood. According to Yamazaki's instruction, the priesthood insists upon inserting the word "carelessly" into Tsuji's statement regarding the so-called wooden Gohonzon incident. A nationwide meeting of priests is held after the Gakkai leaders meeting, after which Nittatsu makes a statement prohibiting priests from further attacking the Gakkai. Active anti-Gakkai priests, however, continue their slander toward the Gakkai and leak a variety of internal information to the tabloid media.

November 14: The priesthood forms its overseas bureau, following Yamazaki's instructions.

January 28: The second Nichiren Shoshu temple members general meeting is held at Taiseki-ji. Active anti-Gakkai priests continue their harsh criticism of the Gakkai. At this meeting, Nittatsu, in a tone rather *1979* critical of the Gakkai, states: "The priests have pointed out the Gakkai's errors and united here with you temple members in order to protect Nichiren Shoshu. Their sincere intent is to widely spread the fundamental spirit of Nichiren Shoshu. I ask that you recognize their profound sincerity. Some priests, however, still remain nonchalant although erroneous teachings have been propagated. Yet so long as they are priests of Nichiren Shoshu, I will protect them magnanimously. I am protecting them as priests of Nichiren Shoshu. I ask for your understanding in this regard. I also ask that you please refute erroneous teachings to the best of your ability . . ." (*Complete Works of High Priest Nittatsu*, vol. 5, part II, pp. 614–15).

March 6: Genjiro Fukushima, then Soka Gakkai vice president, openly criticizes the priesthood at the Omuta Community Center in Fukuoka Prefecture. In his speech,

Fukushima comments: "When President Ikeda goes to the head temple, Gakkai members eagerly greet him, calling him 'Sensei.' But they do not go near the high priest. Nor do they yearn to see him. Even if the high priest walks by, they simply wonder, who is that old man? So priests are jealous and accuse us of treating the president as the true Buddha...." The priesthood is outraged by Fukushima's speech, which has effectively nullified the Gakkai's efforts for reconciliation thus far. (Fukushima later quits the Gakkai and becomes a vehement anti-Gakkai spokesperson, eventually lending support to Nikken.)

March 12: The Nichiren Shoshu Administrative Office submits a letter of inquiry to the Gakkai regarding Fukushima's comments.

March 13: On behalf of Nittatsu, Taiseki-ji's Internal Affairs Department submits a letter of inquiry to the Gakkai regarding Fukushima's comments.

March 31: The Hokkeko Federation (an association of temple parishioners) holds an emergency board of directors meeting and passes a resolution requesting Mr. Ikeda's resignation from the position of chief lay representative.

April 2: Taiseki-ji's Internal Affairs Department, dissatisfied with the Gakkai's response to its initial inquiry, sends another letter of inquiry regarding Fukushima's statements and other matters.

April 6: Mr. Ikeda meets with Nittatsu in hope of restoring harmony. At the meeting, Mr. Ikeda communicates his decision to resign from the position of chief lay representative.

April 8: The Soka Gakkai publishes an apology in the *Seikyo Shimbun* for Fukushima's statements under the name of Hiroshi Hojo, then the general director.

April 24: To resolve the conflict and prevent Gakkai

members from being subjected to further abuse from the priesthood, Mr. Ikeda announces his resignation from the position of Soka Gakkai president at a prefecture leaders meeting. He becomes honorary Soka Gakkai president, and Hiroshi Hojo becomes the fourth Soka Gakkai president. The priesthood asks the Gakkai to no longer allow Mr. Ikeda to attend meetings and to refrain from covering his activities in its daily newspaper, the *Seikyo Shimbun*.

April 26: Mr. Ikeda resigns from the position of chief lay representative of Nichiren Shoshu. Nittatsu appoints him honorary chief lay representative.

May 3: The fortieth Soka Gakkai Headquarters general meeting is held at Soka University in Tokyo. At this meeting, Nittatsu states: "For the last few years, truly regrettable incidents have continued and, to my sadness, have caused confusion. . . . In our Nichiren Shoshu, as you are aware, there are believers who belong to the Hokkeko and other temple groups, as well as to the Soka Gakkai. I ask that all of them be on good terms with one another as believers. Let bygones be bygones. Please cooperate in unity for the development of the priesthood as well as for kosen-rufu" (*Complete Works of High Priest Nittatsu*, vol. 5, part II, pp. 620–21). The closure of the conflict frustrates anti-Gakkai priests, who later become critical of Nittatsu and continue to slander the Gakkai.

May 14: Nittatsu appoints Yamazaki as a lay representative of Nichiren Shoshu along with Soka Gakkai President Hiroshi Hojo, General Director Kazuya Morita, Vice President Satoru Izumi, Vice President Takehisa Tsuji and Vice President Einosuke Akiya. Yamazaki's appointment indicates Nittatsu's great trust in him.

July 22: Nittatsu dies. Shin'no Abe, then general administrator, claims to have received the transmission of the office of high priest from Nittatsu.

August 6: Shin'no Abe renames himself Nikken and becomes the sixty-seventh high priest.

August–September: Yamazaki meets with Nikken several times and recommends that the priesthood continue to undermine the Gakkai membership. Later that September, however, Nikken rejects Yamazaki, calling him a liar. (On January 5, 1991, at the outset of the most recent temple issue, Nikken delivers his apology to Yamazaki for having called him a liar and establishes an alliance with him to attack the Gakkai.)

November: Yamazaki publishes an article in a weekly tabloid, questioning Nikken's legitimacy as high priest. Anti-Gakkai priests, who are mostly Nittatsu's disciples, start to criticize Nikken.

January 9: Nikken asks Mr. Ikeda to issue another apology to silence anti-Gakkai priests, who are critical of Nikken.

March: Yamazaki resigns from the position of chief legal counsel for the Soka Gakkai.

1980

April 2: The *Seikyo Shimbun* publishes an article titled "Reconfirming Our Fundamental Mission" under Mr. Ikeda's name, though he personally did not involve himself or condone its publication. The manuscript has been prepared by the Gakkai leadership at the priesthood's direction. The article reads in part: "It is true that the recent troubles with the priesthood occurred in the wake of the basic policy which the Soka Gakkai adopted for the second phase of kosen-rufu, specifically since 1972 when the Sho-Hondo was completed, and also as a result of guidance which I gave based on that policy during 1977. . . . Now I admit that some of the words I uttered were too self-righteous, too much Soka Gakkai centered, sounding as if the Soka Gakkai were primary and the priesthood secondary. This led some individuals of the priesthood to wonder if the Soka Gakkai might not be contemplating a break with Nichiren Shoshu. It is also true that some of the Gakkai members voiced emotional opinions. I deeply apologize for all this" (May 1980 *Seikyo Times*, pp. 20–22). With this apology published under Mr. Ikeda's name, Nikken attempts to placate anti-Gakkai priests who are questioning the legitimacy of his high office, thus solidifying his position within the priesthood.

April: Yamazaki extorts 300 million yen from the Gakkai in his attempt to bail himself out of large debts created by his failing frozen-food business. Yamazaki threatens Gakkai officials that he will leak more of the Gakkai's internal information to the media and incite weekly tabloids and anti-Gakkai priests to renew their attack on the Gakkai.

June: Yamazaki attempts to extort another 500 million yen from the Gakkai. The Gakkai lodges a complaint with the police.

June: An election is held for the sixteen-member Nichiren Shoshu council. The Shoshinkai, supported by Yamazaki, seeks to gain more than two-thirds of the council; that is, enough votes to change the rules and regulations of Nichiren Shoshu. Sixteen Shoshinkai priests and eight priests from other factions have declared their candidacy. Ten Shoshinkai priests are elected.

July: Anti-Gakkai priests officially form the Shoshinkai.

September: The Gakkai revokes Yamazaki's membership.

1981   **January:** Yamazaki is arrested for extortion. About 180 Shoshinkai priests file a civil lawsuit seeking to revoke Nikken's position as high priest.

1981–   Nikken expels more than 180 Shoshinkai priests,
1983   thus solidifying his position within the priesthood.

1985   **March:** The Tokyo District Court convicts Yamazaki, sentencing him to three years in prison.

APPENDIX B

Chronological List of High Priests

Nichiren Shoshu considers Nichiren Daishonin as its founder, not a high priest. In numbering the successive high priests, however, he is designated as the first.

1	Nichiren Daishonin (1222–1282)	15	Nissho	(1562–1622)
		16	Nichiju	(1567–1632)
2	Nikko Shonin (1246–1333)	17	Nissei	(1600–83)
		18	Nichiei	(1594–1638)
3	Nichimoku (1260–1333)	19	Nisshun	(1610–69)
		20	Nitten	(1611–86)
4	Nichido	(1283–1341)	21	Nichinin	(1612–80)
5	Nichigyo	(n.d.–1369)	22	Nisshun	(1637–91)
6	Nichiji	(n.d.–1406)	23	Nikkei	(1648–1707)
7	Nichia	(n.d.–1407)	24	Nichiei	(1650–1715)
8	Nichiei	(1352–1419)	25	Nichiyu	(1669–1729)
9	Nichiu	(1402–82)	26	Nichikan	(1665–1726)
10	Nichijo	(n.d.–1472)	27	Nichiyo	(1670–1723)
11	Nittei	(n.d.–1472)	28	Nissho	(1681–1734)
12	Nitchin	(1469–1527)	29	Nitto	(1689–1732)
13	Nichiin	(1518–89)	30	Nitchu	(1687–1743)
14	Nisshu	(1555–1617)	31	Nichiin	(1687–1769)

32	Nikkyo	(1704–57)	50	Nichijo	(1795–1836)
33	Nichigen	(1711–78)	51	Nichiei	(1798–1877)
34	Nisshin	(1714–65)	52	Nichiden	(1817–90)
35	Nichion	(1716–74)	53	Nichijo	(1831–92)
36	Nikken	(1717–91)	54	Nichiin	(1829–80)
37	Nippo	(1731–1803)	55	Nippu	(1835–1919)
38	Nittai	(1731–85)	56	Nichio	(1848–1922)
39	Nichijun	(1736–1801)	57	Nissho	(1861–1923)
40	Nichinin	(1747–95)	58	Nitchu	(1865–1928)
41	Nichimon	(1751–96)	59	Nichiko	(1867–1957)
42	Nichigon	(1748–97)	60	Nichikai	(1873–1943)
43	Nisso	(1759–1805)	61	Nichiryu	(1874–1947)
44	Nissen	(1760–1822)	62	Nikkyo	(1869–1949)
45	Nichirei	(1763–1808)	63	Nichiman	(1873–1951)
46	Nitcho	(1766–1817)	64	Nissho	(1879–1957)
47	Nisshu	(1769–1816)	65	Nichijun	(1898–1959)
48	Nichiryo	(1771–1851)	66	Nittatsu	(1902–79)
49	Nisso	(1773–1830)	67	Nikken	(1922—)

Index

219